EMPOWERING CONGREGATIONS

Books by Denton L. Roberts

Able and Equal: A Gentle Path to Peace

Lumps and Bumps:
a Children's Book for Parents and a Parents' Book for Children

Find Purpose—Find Power: Sing the Song in Your Heart

Living as Healer: Everyone Does Therapy and Should Know How

Books by Robert Lee Hill

Made Whole by Broken Bread

We Make the Road by Walking

Hard to Tell

The Color of Sabbath

EMPOWERING CONGREGATIONS

Successful Strategies for 21st Century Leadership

Denton Roberts
and
Robert Hill

Hope Publishing House
Pasadena, California

10/10

For information address:

Hope Publishing House
P.O. Box 60008
Pasadena, CA 91116 - U.S.A.
Tel: (626) 792-6123 / Fax: (626) 792-2121
E-mail: hopepub@telocity.com
Web site: http://www.hope-pub.com

Cover design — Michael McClary/The Workshop

Printed in the U.S.A. on acid-free paper

Library of Congress Cataloging-in-Publication Data

Roberts, Denton L.
    Empowering congregations : successful strategies for 21st century leadership / Denton Roberts and Robert Hill.
        p. cm.
    ISBN 0-932727-98-0 (alk. paper)
    1. Christian leadership. 2. Church growth. I. Hill, Robert, 1952- .
    II. Title.
    BV652. 1 .R62 2003
    253--dc21   2002152862
                                                                        CIP

Contents

Prologue

BILL EMP
The Pastor Who Discovered the Empowering Process

Pastor Bill Emp was in the middle – of age, of raising a family, of his career. As a seasoned professional who realized that both he and the congregation had more potential than they were using, Bill wanted to do something about it. He also knew he was the expert on the congregation. Most importantly, he knew if there were a way to access more power in the situations they faced, he would have to find it.

In the ebb and flow of his routine he seemed to be gradually spending more time in ebb than in flow and he didn't want to continue in that direction. Bill realized many of the tasks he and the congregation faced were mundane, but necessary. For him to launch off into some new scheme without thoroughly preparing himself and his leaders would most probably end in disaster. He had seen this happen to several of his colleagues when the institutional inertia caused then to become desperate for change.

Deepening the sense of community and mission seemed to Bill to be the best way to overcome inertia and transform the mundane. His goal was to make his work a delight instead of a burden. Yet in analyzing his congregational situation he concluded the lethargy he felt didn't seem to be anybody's fault. He just needed some way he could create a greater sense of enthusiasm (flow) and less tedium (ebb) for both himself and the congregation–a way to capture greater passion in the spiritual work they shared.

Bill realized he and his congregation had something in common: they were both gradually shutting down and their zip and zing had gone south. Bill knew he was spending too much time fiddling with items like the bulletin and publications and not enough energy on mission and strengthening spiritual life. Occasionally he had been enthused about projects–like when they computerized the office, but it didn't last very long. More and more it seemed that one day ran into another and one week ran to another and one year ran to another. Aside from periodic crises in his parishioners' lives and occasional in-depth contacts with folks, Bill couldn't seem to recapture his enthusiasm and his idealism had been badly daunted.

As he took the temperature of First Church, in his mind's eye it seemed to Bill it was slowly growing cold and few of the members seemed to have any ideas of what to do or even minded for that matter. Mostly the members acted out of duty and habit rather that a sense of mission and ministry. In his analysis "The church was scratching people where they didn't itch." At the same time Bill was feeling his life was a drift without any clear sense of where he was going or what he was doing.

To deal with his dilemma, Bill sought out a consultant and explained to her where he was in his life and ministry, asking for her help. After hearing him out and determining that he was in good physical and mental health, she said there were lots of things written on ways to make the organization better and to deal with being in the middle of life. She recommended a book on optimal experience–*Flow: The Psychology of Optimal Experience*–and a book on purpose–*Find Purpose–Find Power: Sing the Song In Your Heart*. These books described the conditions necessary to create optimal experience and explained how empowering personal purpose was critical to fulfillment.

In conclusion she said, "Bill, you may just have to create your own book and the guidelines that work for you and First Church."

They agreed to keep in touch.

The consultation wasn't what Bill hoped for, but the idea of making a book on the empowering of First Church gave him a tingle of excitement. He bought the books she had suggested and read them with the idea of creating his own text. As he went through the books, Bill began making a plan to apply the applicable concepts to his life and work.

The *Flow* book had come out of 25 years of research on the necessary conditions conducive to having optimal experience – i.e. happiness and fulfillment. Optimal experience, or "Flow" as it is called, is the state of being so captured by an experience that time and sensation are totally unnoticed. Bill was intrigued to know that optimal experience happens most frequently when people were on task and not when they were on holiday – at work more often than at leisure. Bill decided that he would begin his project by concentrating on how to get more "flow" in his own life. The book *Flow* had given him new insights and he decided his job would be to develop practical ways to create suitable conditions for flow in his daily life.

Find Purpose – Find Power: Sing the Song in Your Heart provided Bill with a process which he could use both in his own life and also introduce to the leaders of the congregation in a modified form. Here he found a model that could be applied to the self, relationships and organizations. It used the cell, the most basic unit of life, as a metaphor for healthy interactions between the self and others.

First Bill decided to concentrate on himself. Long before he had learned from Rabbi Edwin Friedman, a consultant specializing in congregational clergy leadership, that as the clergy leader goes, so goes the congregation. He knew he had to restore his own zip and zing before he could lead the congregation to a new level of vitality. When he was successful himself, he would have plenty of energy and enthusiasm to develop a strategy to empower the congregation.

Empowerment, a highly touted concept for re-energizing organizations, is a complex system that has worked well in business and is now being applied to nonprofit organizations with great enthusiasm but limited success. Bill had been to seminars on applying Quality Management to churches and found it intriguing but difficult to use with a volunteer organization. Nonetheless he thought the concepts had basic merits that could help local congregations.

Bill concluded what he and First Church really needed was empowering before empowerment so he began to think about what kinds of actions were empowering. *Find Purpose-Find Power* had discussed the cycles of success and the cycles of distress and what nourished each of these cycles. He thought if he could use these concepts and systematically apply them to his personal and congregational life he could turn his situation around. The book stressed that understanding, acceptance, praise, realistic expectation and inclusion nourished the cycle of success. Conversely, blame, ridicule, alienation, unrealistic expectations and exclusion fed the distress cycle.

In reading the book Bill had come to understand he was spending way too much time energizing distresses with himself and with the congregation – no wonder he was feeling lousy. He, his peers and the leaders of the congregation were constantly commiserating with one another about the situation in their denomination and the local situation, but actually this activity was not only counter-productive, it was dispiriting.

Bill also knew from his many years as a solo pastor, that it would be easier to set out to animate for change with his empowering project if he had a partner to bounce things off of. He decided to ask Darla, a junior-high principal to be his project partner. Their job responsibilities were similar enough to be comparable and different enough to be contrasting. In the past they both had worked on several boards and committees together, and he had a hunch she'd be interested in learning about "flow" and developing empowering strategies. He hoped the empowerment principles they discovered would be usable to her school as well as to the congregation.

In musing on this plan, Bill noticed he actually was experiencing the feelings described in *Flow*. Great, he thought, the first step in getting more flow and less ebb was to have an exciting project. What was the next step?

Bill had a study leave scheduled and decided to use the time to figure out how he was going to develop his "flow" project. He started by mapping out the basic conditions that created flow for him and made his personal "flow" chart. Step-by-step he analyzed and identified what helped him feel "in the flow." In diagramming how one thing led to another he created Bill Emp's Empowering Map. Then he outlined a process to keep him focused on flow and created Bill Emp's Empowering Target. Finally he developed an Empowering Plan to make sure he used his map and target. As he concentrated on this project, he experienced "flow" more and more of the time and was energized and thinking creative thoughts rather than feeling stuck and concerned with the difficulties in his life work.

After he created the map, target and plan, Bill concluded that in order to succeed with the project he needed support, feedback, reinforcement and encouragement. He had Darla as his project partner, but if others knew and understood his personal map they would be able to provide him support and nourishment and help him when he was off track. So rather than striking out alone, he felt he needed a leadership team with whom he could work close-ly. Rather than make a big deal of it, Bill decided to approach his executive committee and casually tell them what he was wanting to do and what was going on in his life.

Soon after returning from the study leave, Bill scheduled an executive committee meeting to review the status of congregational life. Here he told the others what had been going through his head and then explained to them the project he had designed for himself. Explaining how he thought "flow" could be applied to the congregation, he asked them to join him in this revitalizing experience.

Everyone agreed that more zip and zing would be a boon to the congregation. Bill then went on to explain that as his first step in starting this project he had launched his personal empowering program which was filling him with new hope and enthusiasm and asked if they would support him. His plan, as he outlined it to them, was first to work out the details and dynamics from his personal empowering experiments and as he experienced success, he would use his experience to design a program for empowering the congregation.

He shared his Bill Emp's Empowering Map, Target and Plan with the committee and explained how these practices had helped him re-energize. Passing out copies of his personal map to them, Bill asked the group to mull over these ideas and come back with feedback and insights that came to them.

Sally, the newly elected moderator of the congregation, was an enthusiastic advocate of the plan. She studied Bill's map and let him know she appreciated his sharing his needs and the plans for the specific actions he found enriching, energizing and empowering. "Good," she thought, "with this information I can be more helpful to him and as a bonus I feel I have permission to tell Bill directly what I want and need from him as a person and a leader."

Ted, the chair of the trustees, looked over the Empowering

Map with his normal skepticism and wondered how all this was going to meet the needs of the congregation. He began to suspect Bill had fallen prey to "New-Age-itis" – his term for many of the new trends in the church. But as he dutifully looked at the map, he concluded it wasn't as bad as some of the stuff he had seen.

Fred, the treasurer, was from the old school. "Do your job and keep things on solid ground." He looked over Bill's empowering map and thought, "Well, at least he's one of those who still thinks he can achieve his idealism."

Sue, the junior member of the team, was in charge of community life for the congregation. She was enthusiastic, efficient and liked Bill's sharing. She thought the map was helpful and studied it carefully making out a list of questions for Bill. The empowering process seemed to hold real possibilities for her and if everybody in the congregation began concentrating on producing flow, community life would be great. "This might be just the ticket," she mused.

Life went on. Bill didn't make an overly big deal of his map. However, he personally he used his target faithfully to evaluate his success and to assess what he needed to emphasize in his own life and in his contact with his parishioners. He found by focusing on flow and rating himself daily he felt more in charge of himself. Even some unpleasant tasks seemed more palatable, and he found himself enjoying work more. At least he wasn't "ebbing" as much as before – in fact he getting downright enthusiastic about his job. His contacts were more gratifying and his tasks were more meaningful.

Once or twice in candid conversations Bill mentioned to members of the leadership team some information he had put on his map and how his feelings had changed about his job and the congregation since he had started using this empowering processes. Interestingly, almost every time he brought up his use of the empowering map, target and plan, a meaningful conversation ensued.

Bill made it a point to discuss the details of his project with Darla regularly. Since she was also interested in getting more flow and less ebb in her life and work, they discovered they spent most of their time exchanging exciting ideas. These get-togethers helped both of them stay in flow and focused on empowering.

Between the first and second meeting of the team, Sue and Sally both made a special effort to talk to Bill about his map and the information in it. A couple of times when Bill seemed particularly burdened or particularly enthusiastic, Sue also brought it up. Simply mentioning the map led to meaningful conversations and they realized the map was just as helpful when things were going well as when things were going poorly. Somehow the map helped people empathize and be supportive in the tough times and when things were going well the map made it fun to celebrate success.

Ted asked Bill his purpose in giving the leadership team the map as he thought it was a little unusual for a pastor to lay out his personal needs and preferences so explicitly. Ted told him that on the whole he thought things were going pretty well and he hoped Bill knew he was doing a good job. Bill felt buoyed by Ted's affirmation.

Fred never once mentioned the map. As far as Bill knew Fred never looked at it. However, Fred did his job and seemed comfortable with Bill and regularly complemented him on his sermons.

After a month they held their next meeting. Bill talked about his empowering map and asked if they had found it helpful. Fred and Ted agreed it "hadn't hurt." Ted even conceded it helped him some in knowing how to assist Bill. Sally said she thought it had been a great way to introduce his need for innovation and change. Sue said she felt more allied with Bill and suggested that it would be good for her if she had an empowering map from Fred, Ted and Sally. Having these maps from the others could help them to become more of a team rather than just individual leaders.

Bill had been about to suggest just that as the next step. They agreed to make their own maps and exchange them. Bill saw varying degrees of enthusiasm, ranging from "that's great" to "if you say so, pastor." Each team member made their maps using Bill's format but each did it in their own style. Sally did hers the next day and included a long personal note. Sue took the form home and studied it carefully over the weekend. Ted dashed something off and put a note on the bottom saying he hoped this was enough. Fred waited about a week and handed in a highly detailed, academic-quality piece of work. Bill had the team members' maps duplicated so each had a complete set.

They all studied the others' maps in their own way. Sally found them intriguing and made a list of questions she wanted to ask her teammates. Ted admitted learning some things he had not known about the others. Fred felt the maps might help him work with the others better. Sue thought having the maps made her much more comfortable with the senior members of the team.

During the next month Bill made it a point to review and update his personal map and meet with Darla to talk about how things were going. He studied the team member's maps, keeping them in mind when they were working together. Increasingly Bill became aware of how often he seemed to be in flow. He concluded that just making flow his emphasis helped more than he had imagined.

At the next session Bill shared with the team how he had used the map to develop his Empowering Target, explaining that he was using the target to monitor himself daily. He also admitted that his impetus at the beginning of the project was his feeling caught in the middle with his life ebbing more than it was flowing. Fred and Ted identified with that concern. Bill said developing his project and focusing on flow had helped him get out of that "trapped" feeling.

Sally revealed she had been thinking about giving up her leadership role just before Bill introduced the project because she had felt she just couldn't do what was truly important and concluded she should drop out of leadership. Now she was more hopeful.

Sue had been wondering, she admitted, whether or not her efforts at the church were significant. She, too, seemed to be seeing things differently since they began focusing on flow and empowering. Both Sally and Sue said that identifying their personal purpose and seeing how it was being achieved as they fulfilled the mission of the congregation had been an important step in changing their perspective.

As time went on Bill, Sue, Ted, Sally and Fred developed personal empowering manuals, a team empowering manual and led the congregation in developing a congregational empowering manual. They used these to unify and guide their efforts. They were all astonished at how simple it was.

Introduction

Bill Emp's story, situation and solution serve as metaphors for the dilemmas in a relationship between a congregation and a pastor, as they move from the status quo/business-as-usual/day-to-dayness of congregational life to dynamic and creative ministries relevant to both the life of the congregation and the times in which they live. Bill Emp is every pastor/leader who has learned well how to care for and nurture the life of the congregation and still feels a deep yearning to lead them to new heights effectively.

Congregations that are not empowering are characterized by a certain malaise and lethargy. They are operating more out of ritual than spontaneity – more out of duty rather than joy, while congregations that are empowering are vital and enthusiastic and function with a sense of mission and determination. Empowering congregations emit good vibrations that one feels when one encounters them, just as congregations that are not empowering have a stale ethos that one can't miss when you are among them.

Like all other organizations, congregations have to be open systems and open systems constantly take in nourishment. Such nourishment comes primarily from three sources: 1) spiritual practices (worship, prayer and education); 2) empathetic, sustaining personal relationships; and 3) achievement – fulfilling their mission.

Without vigilance and constant tending, systems have a tendency to close down slowly. As this happens smaller and smaller amounts of nourishment enter the system and lethargy, inertia and routinized activity contaminate congregational life. Bill Emp's tale reflects the insidious beginning of both his and the congregation's system beginning to close down and his pro-active response to dealing with his and the congregation's personal life and mission.

Those who come to use these insights motivated by similar recognitions to Bill's or those who are interested in sharpening their own strategies to keep the systems with which they work open and receiving nourishment must realize that what follows is not a "cookbook" approach to leadership. Instead it is a description of tested and tried strategies that we have used repeatedly throughout our careers to keep ourselves in empowering processes and to build empowering congregations.

WHAT ARE CONGREGATIONS–
Do's and Don't's or Thou's and Thee's?

Congregations are communities of the devout who seek to discern and do the will of the divine. In order to accomplish this task individual members have the implicit responsibility to live in nourishing relationships with both the Creator and the created– each other.

As religious historians, sociologists and congregational practitioners can all attest, congregations on the North American scene have experienced increasing stresses and roadblocks to success. Among mainline Protestant congregations there has been a steady overall numerical decline during the past two generations, accompanied by an equally worrisome loss of morale and purposefulness.

Circumstances are so dire in some denominations that recruitment, training and development of clergy appear to be overwhelmingly daunting tasks. One mainline denomination expects to lose 50% of its clergy leadership–by death, retirement and/or attrition–by the year 2020. In Catholic circles, parishes are ever increasing in size primarily because of the dearth of properly equipped and trained priests. In nearly every expression of Judaism, "outreach" programs abound – because of a necessary focus on institutional stability and/or survival. In evangelical Christian churches, workshops proliferate for leaders and members of congregations who feel besieged, beleaguered and befuddled about appropriate and effective modes for growth and increasing their numbers.

In response to such challenging situations and such crying needs, a stunning array of books and gurus have already offered list upon list of the do's and don't's for congregational success. This is not our purpose here. This book is narrowly focused and concerned with how we create and sustain empowering relationships and congregations. Even the title has a double meaning for *Empowering Congregations* can be understood as generating power in congregations or as creating congregations that empower people. We intend it to be understood both ways. The processes we advocate provide you with skills to discover how to embody both of these meanings. By using the workbook section, you'll begin with focusing on your life purpose and conclude with building a strategy to discern and fulfill the purpose of your congregation.

Our thesis about empowering is plain and straightforward: Nourishing interdependent relationships is the primary source of power placed in the control of humans. Strong positive relationships constantly nourish, stimulate, challenge and empower individuals and, in turn, create empowering communities.

Powerful relationships are nourished and nurtured by what we call "the practice of Thou-ness." This is best understood as the experience of fullness that comes when we are deeply connected to one another – heart to heart, essence to essence, precious to precious. As we look into the eyes of an infant, as we hold the hand of a loved one or friend, as we join in a shared project, as we empathize with another's struggle, as we give and receive support, as we share our joys and deep longings, as we celebrate our victories and triumphs, we practice Thou-ness.

Thou-ness can be characterized as knowing the place where we are called to be. We resonate with Frederick Buechner's telling spiritual metaphor: "The place where God calls you is where your deep gladness and the world's deep hunger meet."

Thou-ness is coming to know another's soul and allowing ourselves to be known on an ever deepening level. Paradoxically, "I cannot know the Thou in Thee unless you reveal it to me, and you cannot know the Thou in me unless I reveal it to Thee." An empowering community is a meeting place where "Thou" and "Thee" exchanges are most likely to occur in mutually nourishing and life-sustaining ways. The practice of Thou-ness is a spiritual exchange, an exchange that affirms, stimulates and brings forth our truest self. In times of deep meaning and true closeness we operate in a "Thou/Thee" paradigm.

We often know the experience of practicing Thou-ness in times of great loss and great victory. However, living in Thou/-Thee relations does not have to be dictated only by happenstance or circumstance. It can also be an intentional act.

On the following pages you will find ways to make the practice of Thou-ness a present and intentional factor in both your personal and congregational life. As you practice Thou-ness you will be living in an empowering posture, fulfilling the place in life that only you can fulfill. As your congregation practices Thou-ness you'll be releasing the power that changes life for the better. Thou/Thee relationships open us to spiritual development in harmony with nature and the divine. Therefore, the better we know and understand the specific actions that empower us and each other, the better we coöperate with the plan of the Creator as we discern it.

The concepts that underlie the process in this book are rooted in the recent discoveries of three social science processes that have been particularly successful in emancipating human potential – the human development theory, quality management practice and the recovery movement. We have found that the discoveries empowering these social sciences, when yoked with individual and congregational spiritual practices, allow individual and communities to develop their unique and dynamic skills for fulfilling mission, personal and institutional.

To guide you in building your empowering skills systematically, we have divided this study into three sections. Section One focuses on personal empowering processes; Two explores how you can apply your personal discoveries to team efforts; and Three looks at creating an empowering ethos throughout your congregation. While these sections necessarily divide empowering into isolated segments, we are aware that success in one area of life affects all other areas.

By making empowering an intentional activity in your personal relationships you'll strengthen your skills in the practice of "Thou-ness." Consequently, you'll be better able to assist yourself, your friends and your colleagues in discovering how to coöperate with the will of the divine. By applying your skills, as developed in these exercises, to your corporate spiritual practices, you'll develop in-depth knowledge of how to fulfill your congregational mission.

As you proceed with the exercises, you'll find the exercises progressively require more and more of your thought and creativity. In that sense the text becomes progressively personal. This is intentional. It is our hope that by the time you have completed this book you will have developed your skills at creating your unique empowering process. Indeed, empowering is an ongoing process that requires increased skill from birth to death.

About the Writers

Denton L. Roberts and Robert L. Hill are clergypersons who have spent their careers empowering and being empowered in and by congregations. They have worked in a variety of churches and church-related social service agencies.

Denton L. Roberts has served in rural, suburban and inner-city pastorates and has been a director of a church and home missions community center in the riot-torn area of South Central Los Angeles. He has had experience in an inter-church counseling center, has been the director of a clergy career counseling center and has directed a community inter-faith organization to overcome racial division.

As a certified teacher in transactional analysis, a licensed marriage family and child therapist and a training consultant for business and organizations, Denton has spent the last two decades developing materials that focus on creating functional human systems (individual, relational and organizational) and in the process has authored four books: *Able and Equal: A Gentle Path to Peace; Lumps and Bumps: A Children's Book for Parents and a Parents' Book for Children; Find Purpose–Find Power: Sing the Song in Your Heart* and *Living as Healer: Everyone Does Therapy and Should–Know How.*

This workbook is a companion piece to *Find Purpose, Find Power (Sing the Song In Your Heart).* By popular demand, he and his colleagues have developed workbooks for applying the ideas contained in his writings to relationships, families, organizations, congregations and businesses and through the Roberts' Leadership Institute (Roberts-institute.com) he is creating an international network that focuses on building healthy functional human systems.

Robert Hill has lengthy experience in social agencies, community service centers and churches in California, Tennessee and Missouri. Not only has he pastored in the inner city and in downtown churches, he has also consulted with congregations in all types of settings–suburban, rural, downtown, inner-urban, urban core, inner-city and college campus and has worked in social service settings dealing with the disenfranchised, the poor and with prisoners and their families.

Through the years, Robert has chaired and provided leadership for numerous social service groups and community organization boards dealing with betterment efforts in race relations, bioethics education, responses to homelessness, hospice care, interfaith understanding, civil rights, community development, alcoholism and drug dependency, international disaster relief, philanthropic foundations and peacemaking. He is much sought after as a keynoter and guest preacher at conferences, retreats, assemblies, ministerial gatherings, festivals and worship services across the United States and has taught seminary courses in the area of preaching. The author of many published articles and poems plus two books, *Made Whole by Broken Bread* and *We Make the Road by Walking,* he also wrote a monthly review column in *The Disciple* magazine.

For the past five years, Denton and Robert have applied the contents of this book to the congregation and staff served by Robert. While success is hard to measure except by mundane statistics, the congregation has grown in every conceivable way and the membership serves the community with an ever-expanding enthusiasm.

While we are both clergy of the Christian faith, we've intentionally written this book with eyes toward eliminating sectarian or theological bias so that it may be used by the devout of all faiths and theological persuasions. By the world's standards our careers are marked by success. We have built and maintained strong, healthy congregations in the city, inner city, suburban and rural settings. We have developed ministries of social outreach from prisons to community organizations, and we have worked with every conceivable socio-economic and ethnic group. We write this not as boasting about our careers, though we are humbly proud of what we have done; rather we write this to show that what we are offering here has passed through the refiner's fire, and we have found ways of dealing effectively with the issues congregations have confronted in the last 40 turbulent years.

The Structure for the Workbook

This workbook involves a step-by-step process and entails a "truth-and-consequences" approach. So step-by-step you will work through the theories and ideas as they unfold, with the ultimate goal of practical application in your congregational relationships. The truths gathered along the way will thus lead to certain welcome and glad consequences. Stories illustrating the theories and ideas are from our experiences of working with real congregations through the years. While the truths of the stories are verifiable, for obvious confidentiality concerns, we have changed the names.

Having met "Bill Emp," the fictionalized clergyperson whose story was in the prologue, you already have an overview of the process. The invented members of Bill's executive committee you no doubt remember from your own life, for they are stereotypical congregational leaders who live and work in every church. So though his tale is fictionalized, anyone familiar with how a typical congregation operates will recognize the accuracy of his story.

The Style of the Workbook

The style of this workbook is Learn, Apply, Create and Teach, and it is designed so that by completing the exercises, participants will be able to develop their own personalized models for empowering – which they can then apply to congregational empowering. Through our experience as leaders of congregations, we recognize the wisdom of the statement: "Hungry parents can't feed children." Our success with congregations has been directly related to our ability to build nourishing relationships within congregations.

Chapter 1

The Case for Empowering

Empowering happens in any spiritual encounter, from individual peak experiences to social spiritual awakenings. It also occurs when the divine and the human meet – whether in human interactions, spiritual practices or peak experiences.

One pastor reports receiving a dream message about the oneness of humanity which came in the form of a poem. Fortunately, the pastor wrote down her dream and recalled later that it was a moment of epiphany, an instance when God seemed to be energizing her life and work. Subsequently she shared the dream with her congregants and they too likened the dream and its poetic written form to a visitation from the divine. Both the pastor and her people expressed gratitude for the dream and for their being able to share it so the dream's impact was invigorating for one and all.

At Community Christian Church in Kansas City, Missouri, the congregation dreamed for years of fulfilling the long-held, yet shelved plans for a "Steeple of Light" which Frank Lloyd Wright had originally posed for the church's unique architecture. Because of World War II "brownouts" at the time the building was constructed in the early '40s and because of the lack of adequate technology to satisfy Wright's original conception, the plans were left on paper.

In 1989 theworld-renowned light sculptor Dale Eldred agreed to build the steeple. He was empowered by the congregation's board to create a design to fulfill what Wright had envisioned. A committee anticipating the congregation's centennial anniversary was particularly enthused about the prospect; however, technological concerns delayed the project.

Finally in 1994, because of Wright's vision, Eldred's design and the hopes and dreams of a persistent congregation, the "Steeple of Light" lit up the skies of Kansas City, beaming star-ward from the church's rooftop dome a 1.3 billion candle-power of illumination, clearly visible for miles around the entire metropolis. An entire community of faith had been energized over decades to "keep on keepin' on."

Wise artists and technicians provided not only appropriate materials and machinery but also attitudes of enlivened coöperation. Citizens throughout a glad and grateful city joined in a large celebration at the time of dedication. In the years that followed, some even suggested the church's towering "Steeple of Light" had become the city's symbol of welcome and hope. Many pointed it out as a sure sign that a benevolent and life-sustaining God was and would remain with Kansas Citians and all who beheld the light. Working together in concert on a common purpose with the shared and renewing power of affirming care and patient hope, a entire community experienced what one person described as "the touch of the divine."

These two illustrations demonstrate how empowering experiences can happen in congregations, sometimes starting with a pastor, others originating with a group's abiding hopes, as in the case of the "Steeple of Light." We might posit that empowerment happens at the intersection of "Humanity Highway" and "Divinity Drive." When we allow the possibilities for such an intersection to be constructed, or better yet, when we actively, purposefully pursue the construction of such an intersection, the empowering process abounds. And hearts are glad. And, to quote Tony Campolo, "It's party time!"

Nurture and Issue Considerations

The many considerations with which a congregation must contend fall under two major headings: *nurture* and *issue*. Nurture considerations (pastoral) have to do with the care of body, soul and relationships. Issue considerations (mission) have to do with the care of organizations, institutions and the social order.

In congregational life, we care for nurture and issue considerations either directly or indirectly – consciously or unconsciously. Empowered people and congregations have learned to meet human and societal needs (nurture and issue considerations) effectively. When we observe such people we call them saints and the congregations we term powerful and effective.

Faith communities are ordained to unify our efforts and stimulate our spiritual growth. Ideally, faith communities provide nurturing environments and relationships. These communities create a stable social order in our families, organizations and on the planet. Though beliefs, dogmas and rituals may vary, the effectiveness of any congregation is ultimately determined by how well nurture and issue considerations are met.

In this age of complexity, the need to be effective at caring for our own and for our fellow seekers' nurture and issue considerations is critical to success. To the extent we develop our skills in meeting nurture and issue considerations, we contribute our gifts and build the kind of community our faith traditions espouse and value most highly. With these communities, we shape a social order that is harmonious with our highest values.

Building Community

The challenge for a congregation is to build continuously a community that empowers – a community where the major portion of energy is directed toward "equipping the saints" to fulfill their mission; where precious historical identity is treasured, but not worshiped; where creativity and discovery are nurtured and where harmony and mutual support are the rule. The challenge to build such a community is met directly and indirectly – intentionally and accidentally – throughout congregations of all religions day-by-day and year-by-year.

Community seldom comes about by accident. Recent studies by M. Scott Peck (*Further Along the Road Less Traveled*) identify that there are processes by which community is built and individual gifts and skills are nourished as our aspirations are actualized. Understanding and mastering these processes are key to fulfilling both our individual and congregational missions.

On the pages that follow we synthesize some of the discoveries of human development psychology, quality management practices and the recovery movement. The insights discovered by these social sciences are translated into common-sense processes you can apply to your leadership skills to fulfill your personal and congregational mission better.

By mastering and applying some of the simple wisdom these fields offer, we are not suggesting that congregations should be run like a psychological laboratory, a business or a self-help movement. But rather as we adapt these insights and apply them to congregational leadership, we can unlock new dimensions of personal and congregational potential.

What Do We Mean by Empowering Process?

Power means "able to." Process is "a series of continuous actions that brings about a particular result or end." An empowering process is a series of actions that results in enabling self and others, individually and collectively, to achieve a desired result or end – to fulfill mission. As people of faith, our desired end is to care for nurture and issue considerations in such a way that life is lived as it was intended – the rule of love in the hearts of humans.

The growth of the number of young families with young children in the St. James congregation presented a challenging dilemma to the pastor and her people. There was an obvious lack of adequate and equipped staff to provide the nurture, education and training that so many new young families needed. Although the swelling numbers of young parents with small children were impressive and an obvious change from the years of inactivity and stagnation that had preceded the time of new growth, the needs of this burgeoning congregation also stimulated a sense of uncertainty that in some people bordered on panic.

In some of the congregations in which some of the newer families had previously been members, new growth had been met by old resistances. When new growth had occurred in those previous contexts, lack of appropriate funding and encrusted patterns of leadership stifled the newness and eventually the old status quo returned. Despite the excitement of the new growth, the St. James people were fearful such a pattern would settle in with them.

Fortunately, the pastor and the congregational leaders at St. James decided to enter into a process of discussion and dreaming and make an adventure out of their dilemma. They created a "Dream Team" group to address the challenges of the new growth intentionally. Instead of approaching the growing needs for appropriate religious education as daunting problems, the Dream Team took this on as an exciting opportunity.

Eventually the Dream Team decided to plan a nine-month schedule of discussions, retreats and round-table talks. At the end of this time they had forged a prioritized "Wish List" for programming, materials, equipment and staff needs. Over the next three years, all of the "Wish List" items were realized at St. James, with each fulfillment inspiring new hope, new resources (financial and personal) and new energy for the next steps of growth.

The key to the St. James success story was summed up by one of the venerable "old guard" leaders who had caught the vision of the new process and the new way of meeting challenges in the ever-expanding congregation: "Our previous habit of saying no to everything didn't seem to be the answer any of us, especially the younger people, would accept. With our pastor leading the way, we waded into the trouble and discovered it to be a sho-nuff, bonafied adventure. Besides, it was a hoot and we always seemed to come up with enough money and people to do the job that needed to be done."

Why Consider Developing an Empowering Strategy?

We all possess both natural and learned skills which range from spiritual practices to counseling, from building community to creating happy families. Our skills are both unconscious habits and conscious strategies.

Habits are the ingrained actions we automatically take without conscious thought. Frequently these work well and produce the desired result. However, when we are not achieving the goals we'd like, even though our actions are well intended, it is a good idea to reëxamine our habits, for there is indeed a difference between our intent and our impact. It is not unusual for a congregational leader to have good intent with a leadership habit that proves to have a debilitating impact on the community.

Jane was the leader of a congregation struggling to select a new minister. She frequently confronted her committee and the congregation asking, "What do you people want?" Her intent was to be inclusive and democratic, but instead she alienated her congregation because they felt she was talking down to them. Until she reëxamined her modus operandi and changed it, her style proved counter-productive to her leadership role.

Strategies are well-developed plans that take into consideration both intent and impact as we move to a clearly defined outcome. Once Jane became aware her intent and impact were at cross-purposes, she modified her strategy and began to ask her groups if her actions were acceptable to the group as she introduced each proposed action and asked for input from them. As her habits changed and she adopted a conscious strategy her intent and impact became congruent. Her experience of leadership became a joy for her and she received the kind of support she needed to perform her difficult assignment.

Habits and strategies determine the outcome because they create the environments that shape us all. While rebuilding the Parliament buildings in England after World War II, Winston Churchill argued successfully for rebuilding traditional buildings rather than modern, "efficient buildings." His logic was, "we shape our buildings and after that they shape us. " Developing our empowering skills rests on the same logic. We create our empowering processes and, once developed, our processes shape us.

Empowerment and Empowering

This book is about empowering not empowerment even though empowerment tends currently to be an "in" word. This concept came into vogue from the field of business management. In business circles it is a highly technical process.

Empowering is the process of providing the tools to achieve desired outcomes effectively. Technically speaking, empowerment is the process of placing decision-making authority in the hands of those persons who most directly deal with the problem and who will be most affected by the outcome.

We have come to realize that empowering needs to be understood and mastered before empowerment can be effective – especially in volunteer organizations like churches, synagogues, mosques and temples. You might compare empowering like the process of learning to ride a bicycle whereas empowerment is like using the bicycle to get where you want to go. Empowering is the process we use to get to empowerment.

While there is always a need for empowerment within congregations, our experience shows that empowering is a necessary first step before empowerment can be achieved effectively. The processes that follow in this book are designed to help you develop empowering skills. These skills will both help you fulfill your personal mission and at the same time will create an environment that people want to be a part of because it helps them to fulfill their mission as it also provides them with skills to cope with life dilemmas.

Empowering Discoveries

The text and exercises that follow synthesize the insights of:
1. Human development theory;
2. Quality management practice; and
3. The recovery movement.

Human development theory focuses on how people naturally develop and what needs have to be met in order to become healthy and autonomous adults. Quality management focuses on how organizations operate in order to produce quality products and services. The Recovery movement focuses on what people need to do and have in order to recover from the wounding of destructive addictions and behaviors.

Pulling together and applying the information and insights of these three recently developed processes can greatly help us meet the many diverse demands of a congregation.

Human Development

From psychological and human development research we learn that the natural way people are empowered is in healthful interdependent relationships. Through the regular repetition of the cycle of attachment, bonding, separating and individuating, we grow and develop. In this cycle, attachment and bonding relate to being available and dependable resources to one another. Separating and individuating relate to standing alone and defining the self. In child development theory, each successful completion of this cycle empowers, but each unsuccessful completion of this cycle results in some degree of wounding.

We would suggest this natural, healthful empowering sequence is not limited to child development. Throughout all of life from birth to death the regular repetition of this cycle provides essential emotional sustenance and builds self-esteem (confidence and competence). The better we understand and learn to advance this natural growth cycle in human relations, the more likely we are to achieve our goals.

Further, we suggest that all human systems – from partnerships to volunteer organizations – naturally advance by the repetition of the cycle of attachment/bonding/separating/individuating. This is easily observed in courtship, marriage and growing in relationship. A sustained relationship reflects this cycle with each developing stage of life.

Such a cycle is not as easily observed in a voluntary faith community but it is there nonetheless. A person is attracted by a faith and a particular congregation, they attach and bond. After the attachment and bonding phase is successfully completed they offer their talents and skills in serving the congregation. In the next phase they offer their unique/creative leadership, i.e. they separate and individuate. This cycle continues as they grow in "wisdom and stature and favor" with God and their fellow seekers. As long as the cycle is supported they are both empowered and empowering in both their personal and congregational life. Failure to advance the cycle from attachment to individuation in either a marriage or a congregation results in a stagnation in growth in the particular area where the cycle is not completed.

Quality Management

From quality management, frequently identified as TQM, we learn that excellence is produced when an entire organization: 1)

Focuses on a common purpose; 2) Strives toward continuous improvement; and 3) Is unified and guided by explicit principles. In other words excellence is purpose-focused, improvement-oriented and principle-managed.

In professional circles W. Edwards Deming is known as the progenitor of quality science and is credited as one of the most important architects in the rebuilding of the Japanese industrial complex following World War II. Before Deming and Quality Management (TQM), the label "Made in Japan" often was thought of as a shoddy inferior product. Since Deming and the quality revolution, the same label came to be regarded as a sign of quality.

A little-known fact about Dr. Deming is that he was a committed church person who, no doubt, was influenced in developing his considerable insight into quality management processes by his religious training and belief.

The three key concepts of his method are:

1. Maintain constancy of purpose (Purpose-focused)
2. Focus on continuous improvement (Improvement-oriented)
3. Manage organizations by agreed-upon principles (Principle-managed)

We do not have to contemplate long these basic concepts before we perceive the spiritual nature that underlies them. Indeed congregations of all faiths operate, however clumsily, by allegiance to a common purpose, growing in understanding of the faith and/or organization and fidelity to basic tenets. Constantly focusing on purpose means keeping "mission" (organizational and individual) in our sights at all times. Focusing on continuous improvement keeps us refining our gifts, talents, skills and abilities. Managing by principles involves making daily decisions consistent with our deepest beliefs. (You can imagine what congregational life is like when every member utilizes this formula to fulfill the mission of the congregation.)

Recovery

From the recovery movement we learn that redemptive empowering occurs in networks that provide:
1. A sense of belonging;
2. A community that affirms;
3. Relationships that foster mastery and excellence; and
4. Relationships that nourish and reward achievement and fulfillment.

The recovery movement has created healing and empowering environments by providing these essentials for people trapped in the continuously wounding web of self-destructive and addictive behaviors. Recovery programs have effectively redeemed people struggling with almost every known addiction. Frequently, the recovery programs like Alcoholics Anonymous and Narcotics Anonymous have been successful at facilitating recovery and healing where professional efforts have failed. Recovery has been successful because they have succeeded at providing the very essentials of congregational life.

The techniques rediscovered, developed and applied by these three fields of specialization are nothing new to us in spiritual communities. Effective congregations have done all these things throughout the years; however, for various reasons, congregations have frequently lost sight of these functions. By consciously and intentionally applying these insights, congregations can develop powerful tools to help them develop clear-cut strategies for fulfilling their mission purpose. In this complex, high-speed era, intentionally concentrating on developing an in-depth understanding and applying successful processes of empowering helps us reclaim our energy to do what we are commissioned to do efficiently and effectively.

Diamond was an African-American woman who came to First Church because it was one of the few in the area that would accept her inter-racial family. As a seven-year member of Alcoholics

Anonymous, she had much to offer the congregation and the congregation offered her much. However, once she and her family had attached and bonded to the congregation and after they had moved into leadership roles, Diamond realized the nourishment she received in the congregation did not compare to what she received in AA.

While attending one of our empowering workshops where these three successful concepts were presented she quickly identified what was missing for her. Rather than get upset with the congregation for its limitations, she asked if she could start a group for those who felt the need for more nourishment than the traditional congregational activities provide. Soon she had a lively group meeting weekly in the church parlor. During the following years this "personal support group" multiplied until there were five such gatherings and the pastor always had a place to send the lonely, hurting people he counseled. People brought their friends, the church grew and the mission of the congregation expanded in a way that provided a real feeling of fulfillment throughout the congregation.

If Diamond had not had a concept that allowed her to identify what was missing for her and if the congregation had not been open to expanding their own processes, she may have settled for what the congregation had to offer. (Or, as we all know, far too often congregations seem to scratch where people don't itch. When people don't get what they are looking for, they simply resign themselves to accepting what's available or leave.) However, since the congregation was intentional about empowering, Diamond was able to give her gift, offering her unique skills in a way that both she and the congregation expanded and thereafter, fulfilled a new mission.

A hallmark of an empowering congregation is people giving and receiving what they want rather than settling for what they can get.

Application

The exercises that follow are based on a synthesis of the insights of human development, quality management and recovery to create a non-technical, "commonsense/user-friendly" approach to individual, team and congregational empowering. As you complete the exercises you will find that you will also be developing your own unique models for individual, team and congregational empowering tailored to your current situations. The exercises will help you create your personal map, target and plan. What you end up with will be your own empowering creation.

Commitment

To become expert at empowering takes commitment. A light reading of this material will give you some bright ideas – which may be all you want or need. However, we recommend you read through the entire text quickly to get the big picture. Then go back and work through the exercises over a period of time. Also, we have found that if at all possible, it is most helpful to do the exercises with a partner like Bill Emp did. This material is most effectively mastered if you make a commitment to complete the exercises step-by-step. To understand why such a commitment is essential we invite you to do the following exercise.

"Thumbs Up"

Clasp your hands in front of you, lacing your fingers as you would normally. Be aware of how comfortable it feels and notice which thumb is on top. Now unclasp your hands and clasp them again, lacing your fingers together in a deliberately opposite fashion, placing the other thumb on top. Notice how strange they feel.

If you knew for sure or had a strong indication that your life would improve if you put the "other" thumb on top each time you clasped your hands, at first out of habit you would probably still do it in the old, familiar way. However, if you were committed to learning to put the other thumb on top and consciously reminded yourself to do so, over a period of time it would become familiar, comfortable and eventually automatic. Developing your conscious empowering model is like learning which thumb to put on top.

Currently, like all human beings, you have developed effective, semi-effective and ineffective habits. By coming to an in-depth understanding of the empowering process you currently use, you will be better able to integrate these new insights to make the semi-effective and ineffective models effective. As a bonus, you'll also come to understand better why your effective models are so.

Competency

Developing mastery and becoming competent at empowering is like becoming a professional musician, athlete or master craftsperson – all require regular study, practice and performance. Through learning, practice and performance, talents and skills are successfully refined. Competent professionals in these fields spend several hours a day in practice to hone their skills. Empowering requires the same dedication and perseverance. Therefore to be empowering, you need to apply your learning daily. This is not difficult for each situation you encounter provides an opportunity to exercise your empowering skills.

Empowering behaviors are to the spiritual person what seeing is to a photographer, listening is to a musician, or training is to an athlete. Just as you may have consciously developed step-by-step processes to give comfort to the grieving or prepare a budget, so pastors need to develop processes to empower themselves and the people in their life and faith community. As Tex Sample, seminary professor of social ethics and theology and a leader in the field of church demographics and societal change, has shown, it is only by regular practice that behaviors become competencies.

For the past 25 years Denton Roberts has been involved in an organization that developed a competency-based training program of counselors, educators, therapists and organizational development experts. Competency-based training differs from academic training because it's been discovered that as people gain both *information* and *application* in equal proportions in the learning process, they become competent practitioners. Emphasizing just one of these components and neglecting to give equal attention to the other may not produce competency – which involves both knowledge and practical application.

The processes that follow are based on a succinct formula: learn it – apply it – create it – teach it. As you complete the following sections, you will be creating your own tailor-made empowering process. Plus, you'll notice your skills at empowering improve from the very beginning.

Personal Empowering

Chapter 2

Empowering: The Process for Congregations

Gentle with Self / Flowing in Relationships / Creative in the World

Several years ago Denton Roberts was asked to lead a retreat for Protestant clergy on "Fulfilling Your Call." After the opening session, the group expressed some discomfort with his approach saying they wanted to know his goals. They had come to what was supposed to be a "spiritual" retreat and they were feeling that Roberts' approach was more organizational and developmental than they expected.

Without considering the challenge too long, Roberts replied that his goals for the retreat were the same as his goals as a pastor, counselor and parent. He wanted to share with them empowering processes to help them be gentle with themselves, flowing in their relationships and creative in the world.

Being gentle with self meant exercising the same quality of compassion, nurture and understanding in their actions toward themselves as they did in their pastoral considerations for their parishioners. Flowing in relationships meant interacting with consistency, negotiating conflicts and moving from one focus to another as they strove to fulfill their mission. Being creative in the world meant discovering afresh each day what they had to contribute to the fulfillment of their faith.

As time passed, Roberts realized this rather hurried response was a good synopsis of empowering. Gentle with self, flowing in relationships and creative in the world sums up the state of well-being that allows us to pursue our goals vigorously.

Consciously and unconsciously, we yearn for warm, deep and meaningful experiences – those optimal experiences Bill Emp identifies as "flow." The Psalmist describes such experiences with phrases like "*Such knowledge is too wonderful for me ...*" In contemporary parlance we might hear, "*It doesn't get any better than this.*" However said, we humans long to feel this flow as much as possible.

It would be naïve to think that we can live perpetually in such a state of grace, yet it is a healthy desire and a worthy target. Mastery of the empowering process helps us create communities that support and target this state of being as we go about our day-to-day activities fulfilling our mission – personal and organizational. On the highest level the mission of a congregation is to empower good and dis-empower evil. As we strive to achieve this mission, the better we know precisely how to optimize individual and congregational power, the better off we are.

Why Create an Empowering Manual?

You begin by building a personal empowering manual – by which you will be better able to monitor and guide your efforts. Later you will build your own leadership team and congregational empowering manuals – by which you will design and implement with your congregation's mutually agreed-upon ways of addressing your mission. With these manuals you can create a way to unify your efforts and actions so you are all "reading off the same page" as you identify and fulfill your mission.

Mastering the empowering processes in this text shepherds you in building your personal, team and congregational empowering manuals. Once built, these manuals serve as guides that allow you to address the *nurture* and *issue* considerations of your individual and collective lives and thus serve to keep your systems open and nourishing and remove the threat of your systems shutting down.

Why Are Empowering Manuals Necessary?

When someone in the commercial world buys a new piece of equipment it comes with a manual of operating instructions. When the equipment is put into service or whenever it malfunctions, the owner refers to the operating manual. This is not so with congregations and/or congregational members. Neither congregations nor individuals come with operating manuals. When members or groups within congregations function inadequately, experience conflict or cast about for a sense of direction, leaders and fellow members are often at a loss for how to nourish them. They are left wondering what can be done to help them "get up to speed" and "on line," restoring harmony, balance and reaching full productivity.

Given that human beings are infinitely more complex than machinery, the need for explicit information on how to support and motivate optimal functioning is critically important. Knowing how to comfort in grief, inspire in times of discouragement, create plans to fulfill mission and address the forces that threaten our most precious beliefs effectively is something we all must master. A manual of "operating instructions" for the empowering process is, we believe, just the ticket!

Shortly before Denton's first grandson was born he gave his son and daughter-in-law a copy of Anne Lamott's *Operating Instructions*. This humorous and realistic story of her experience as a new mother scraped away all the idealistic sentimentality of parenting and in beautiful prose offered a realistic rendering of what it is like to be a first-time parent during the first three years of a child's life. As time passed these new parents made it a point to express thanks for this book of operating instructions. It helped them nourish themselves and each other as they forayed into this new adventure.

Empowering manuals will help you, your leadership team and your congregation maintain nourishing systems just as it helped

Bill Emp, his team and congregation. The interactive process of this workbook outlines a method for empowering through creating manuals that allow you to create:

- Your personal empowering maps, targets and plans (maps set the course, targets keep you focused and plans provide a logical sequence of action);
- Outlines for leading others in creating personal empowering manuals;
- Processes for creating team and congregational empowering manuals; and
- Plans for implementing congregational empowering.

The following assessment will give you an overview of the components you will explore. Fill them in quickly and intuitively.

Personal Assessment
(Mark your internal degree of satisfaction)

1. Is my life purpose clear?

0% _____ 25% _____ 50% _____ 75% _____ 100% _____
(UNFULFILLED)   (FULFILLED)

2. Are my needs for personal support being met?

0% _____ 25% _____ 50% _____ 75% _____ 100% _____
(UNFULFILLED)   (FULFILLED)

3. Is the mutual respect I experience with others adequate?

0% _____ 25% _____ 50% _____ 75% _____ 100% _____
(UNFULFILLED)   (FULFILLED)

4. Do I have a sense of pride in achievement?

0% _____ 25% _____ 50% _____ 75% _____ 100% _____
(UNFULFILLED)   (FULFILLED)

5. Am I (emotionally, intellectually, physically and spiritually) safe?

0% _____ 25% _____ 50% _____ 75% _____ 100% _____
(UNFULFILLED)   (FULFILLED)

6. Are the positive connections I experience with others sufficient?

0% _____ 25% _____ 50% _____ 75% _____ 100% _____
(UNFULFILLED)   (FULFILLED)

7. Is my communication clear?

0% _____ 25% _____ 50% _____ 75% _____ 100% _____
(UNFULFILLED)   (FULFILLED)

8. Are my activities productive?

0% _____ 25% _____ 50% _____ 75% _____ 100% _____
(UNFULFILLED)   (FULFILLED)

9. Are my celebrations re-creating my vigor for the tasks ahead?

0% _____ 25% _____ 50% _____ 75% _____ 100% _____
(UNFULFILLED)   (FULFILLED)

Congregational Assessment

Instructions: (Answer for your congregation in your opinion)

1. Is our congregational purpose clear?

0% _____ 25% _____ 50% _____ 75% _____ 100% _____
(UNFULFILLED)   (FULFILLED)

2. Are the support needs of the congregation being met?

0% _____ 25% _____ 50% _____ 75% _____ 100% _____
(UNFULFILLED)   (FULFILLED)

3. Is the mutual respect experienced in the congregation adequate?

0% _____ 25% _____ 50% _____ 75% _____ 100% _____
(UNFULFILLED)   (FULFILLED)

4. Is there a sense of pride in achievement throughout the congregation?

0% _____ 25% _____ 50% _____ 75% _____ 100% _____
(UNFULFILLED)   (FULFILLED)

5. Does safety (emotional, intellectual, physical and spiritual) exist for all the congregation members?

0% _____ 25% _____ 50% _____ 75% _____ 100% _____
(UNFULFILLED)   (FULFILLED)

6. Are the positive connections expressed in the congregation adequate?

0% _____ 25% _____ 50% _____ 75% _____ 100% _____
(UNFULFILLED)   (FULFILLED)

7. Is our communication open?

0% _____ 25% _____ 50% _____ 75% _____ 100% _____
(UNFULFILLED)   (FULFILLED)

8. Are our activities productive?

0% _____ 25% _____ 50% _____ 75% _____ 100% _____
(UNFULFILLED)   (FULFILLED)

9. Are our congregational celebrations re-creating our strength for the tasks at hand?

0% _____ 25% _____ 50% _____ 75% _____ 100% _____
(UNFULFILLED)   (FULFILLED)

(This assessment owes a large debt to Scott Peck and his *The Road Less Traveled* and *Trauma and Recovery.*)

Chapter 3

Your Role in Empowering

A current medical brochure of an insightful HMO makes a startlingly clear declaration: "The most important member of your medical team is yourself." No one can argue with that. The same is true for your empowering team. You begin the process of empowering with yourself by creating your personal empowering manual. This involves:

- identifying your purpose
- building positive alliances
- establishing interpersonal bridges

How to Best Use this Workbook

Since you most likely came to this book because of your concern for congregations, you are best served to begin by focusing on yourself. While you probably have many insights into your relationships and congregational life, we have found these insights, although inspiring, can also be distracting. Thus we recommend you keep a separate notebook or personal diary to write down these inspirations and ideas. Later these will be quite useful.

You'll be surprised by how much you already know about empowering your congregation. However, the object of this process is to organize first what you know about what empowers you. Once you know what empowers you and have it well in your conscious mind and are comfortable to speak of it freely, you are ready to share your insights in team- and congregation-building. Launching into team and congregational work before you have personally been through the exercises can be confusing, even self-defeating.

We've also found when you work with your team and congregation after you first understand fully what empowers you, your chances of success and fulfillment are much greater.

The Importance of Purpose

Purpose is critical to the optimal functioning of any of the many systems in which you operate – individual, relational or organizational. Purpose is critical because it provides focus and direction. It is also the central unifying goal that directs our actions, guides decisions and ultimately provides meaning. Purpose in life for the spiritual person is something we discern through our myriad of life experiences – planned and unplanned. It matters little whether our current activity is routine or lofty, when we know our purpose the experience becomes an adventure.

Anyone who watches two-year-olds go about their daily play and discovery, can easily see that when they have a purpose in mind they are totally focused and intense. It is only when they lose focus and do not have a purpose in mind that you can observe them wandering about aimlessly looking for something else to catch their attention. Obviously they are much more focused when they have a purpose – and consequently they are also much happier then.

Victor Frankl, father of Logo Therapy/Meaning Therapy and a survivor of the death-camp at Auschwitz developed his whole therapeutic philosophy based on the observation that those who survived this terrible ordeal were those who kept focused on their purpose. His small book *Man's Search for Meaning* is based on Nietzsche's maxim: "He who has a why for living can endure almost any how."

We cannot minimize the importance of purpose to the well-being and survival of individual human life. This is also true for institutional life.

It matters little whether we believe in divine destiny or total free will, purpose must be discerned for life to be meaningful. The poet Antonio Machado put it this way: "*Se hace camino al andar.*" Roughly translated in English: "We make the road by walking."

What Are Positive Alliances?

Some years ago our friend Joe was responsible for heading up a fund-raising campaign to build a new church building. A professional consultant had advised him the goal for the campaign was too high and that he would have to give a powerful speech for this not to turn out to be an embarrassing failure.

His presentation was simple. Joe said, "We all want to do something significant with our life. Sooner or later most of us realize that very few of us can do it alone. However, when we work together we can do great things."

That was the entirety of his speech. We passed out the pledge cards and when we tallied the results the total was double our goal. What Joe had stated – that we all know – was when we are connected in a common cause, we can succeed at fulfilling our purpose.

Positive alliances refer to how we healthfully attach and bond in order to be resources for one another and accomplish mutual goals. Studies show that successful relationships have three primary qualities which create positive alliances: 1). warmth/support, 2). empathy/mutual respect, and 3). self-disclosure/discovery. When these qualities are abundantly present in relationships, they allow people to grow, develop and ultimately find and fulfill their purpose.

Right after the Los Angeles uprising which occurred in response to the court case over the beating of Rodney King, Robert

Hill was asked to lead the Greater Kansas City Metropolitan Human Relations Commission. Representatives from the 14 largest municipalities in the area came together to seek ways of understanding and coöperation across divisions of racial separation in order to prevent anything similar from happening in Kansas City.

Significant time was allotted during the Commission's initial meetings for making positive connections among the representatives. Many of the members of the group were church leaders who were given a chance to interact with one another and share stories of their congregations over several lunch gatherings. It took six months for the Commission to complete a clear and straightforward mission statement, but during that period each municipality's representative gave warm assent and consistent respect to the other members and their particular concerns.

While the "preparatory" work of getting to know one another over these lunches seemed to take a long time, it paid off in the long run because the members could work together harmoniously. After the mission statement was affirmed and celebrated among all the communities represented around the Commission's table, programs promoting tolerance, sensitivity and understanding were quickly enacted for elementary school children, high school youth and adults. More than 250,000 people and their families were affected by the work of the Commission during its five-year tenure. The careful work of creating positive alliances resulted in tremendous dividends for an entire metropolis.

What Are Interpersonal Bridges?

Positive alliances form the infrastructure necessary to build "interpersonal bridges" – a term that comes from psychotherapy. Clinicians recognize that in order to be helpful they first have to form a trustable positive alliance. Once this is formed, clinicians systematically build interpersonal bridges so that they can exchange information and experience freely.

"Interpersonal Bridge" is a metaphor for how the commerce of empowering is carried on between people. Such bridges symbolize the connections that make possible the exchange of the vital commodities that psychologically and spiritually nourish us. In child development studies, an interpersonal bridge is used to denote the process of attachment, bonding, separating and individuating. While these terms have great technical significance they may not have much immediate meaning for the average person. In practical and less technical terms, an interpersonal bridge is built between people by creating safety, developing positive connections, maintaining open communication, participating in productive activity and sharing in rewards/celebration.

This cycle – which begins with the creation of safety, advances to making a positive connection which leads to open communication which clears the path for productive activity which ultimately leads to rewards and celebration – is the natural cycle that creates success. In order for an interpersonal bridge to carry the commerce of empowering all of these elements must be potential or present in relationships.

Instructions: On the following pages you will find exercises that relate to the empowering process generally and your personal empowering process in particular. Complete the exercises quickly and off the top of your head. On completing this section you will have built your personal empowering target, map and plan. With these you can monitor your personal empowering needs.

Purpose

"To love someone is to learn the song in their heart and to sing it to them when they have forgotten it." – Anonymous

This quotation is a poetic expression of empowering in relationship. It is inspiring because it encapsulates the natural way human beings exchange support and can restore balance in life. Singing the song in your heart is a metaphor for fulfilling your purpose. Your song needs to be brought out, made explicit and shared. In daily life you may or may not bear in mind the song in your own heart. You may not be aware of the songs in the hearts of others. However, knowing your song is crucial to creating an empowering relationship with others and ourselves. When another knows the song in your heart and sings it to you, you feel nourished. When you know someone's song and sing it to them, you are nourishing. Paradoxically it is nourishing to the human soul to provide nourishment to another.

Your song is a result of the blending of your unique (genetic) make-up and your life experiences. Your empowering process begins with detecting and articulating it. Ancient myths tell us that if we can name the monster, we can conquer it. The same logic applies here: If you can articulate your song, you can sing it. As others learn your song and you learn theirs, you can create an antiphonal chorus that mutually nourishes as you and they encounter the vicissitudes of life.

As you concentrate on identifying your purpose, you develop an in-depth knowledge of your song. As you focus on your song, you'll naturally nourish it and create internal harmony. This harmony is much like what you have with a "bosom buddy." As you share your song with others, you'll invite harmonic resonance with them.

Harmonic resonance is a term for that feeling of being-in-sync with yourself, with someone else, with life itself. Harmonic resonance is called intimacy. Years ago while Denton was supervising a group of beginning Ph.D. interns, one particular participant was having great difficulty feeling what she did had any real value. Finally Denton challenged her to confront herself with the question of whether or not she believed she was lovable.

"Am I willing to believe that I am lovable?" was the question she was to ask herself whenever doubts of her effectiveness arose — and do this regularly for the next month. When she returned to the group, she reported, "I've had this strange feeling. The best I can describe it is 'cozy with myself' and I've felt that my work was productive."

What she had done was stimulate her own harmonic resonance. With her "cozying" up to herself, she was better able to connect with her clients. This aptly illustrates the power of harmonic resonance – and knowing your song leads to harmonic resonance.

The clearer your purpose ("song") becomes, the greater your internal harmony and the better you'll understand how it resonates with the purposes of others. When you are in harmonic resonance with yourself and others, you feel good and live in what theologians call "a state of grace." Life is meaningful, though not always pleasant and easy, as in the closeness felt in grief and the bondedness felt in struggle.

Focusing on purpose does the same for your empowering as developing an "eye" does for the photographer or developing an "ear" does for the musician. It trains you to see and hear excellence and to improve your performance constantly. You'll discover that your understanding of your life purpose emerges like a blossoming flower. At first when you focus on purpose it may not be crystal clear. As you proceed with these exercises, content yourself with your intuitive sense of purpose, "your purpose for now."

The more thought and attention you give to purpose, the clearer it becomes. We've found as you keep your purpose before you, you gain ever increasing clarity. Purpose is elusive and something we detect. Perhaps it is never crystal clear. Be content with temporary/ imperfect answers as you do the following exercise.

Exercise

Off the top of your head write your life purpose in 25 words or less. By doing this off the top of your head you access the intuitive part of you. By reviewing your purpose regularly your purpose becomes increasingly clear. If you have difficulty getting started, answer the following questions to stimulate your memory:

- In late adolescence, as you entered the adult world, what were your dreams for the good life?
- Imagine yourself in old age looking backwards and assessing your life and then ask yourself "How did I make my life count? For what do I want to be remembered?"
- List three achievements in life you are most proud of. What do these have in common? What do they tell you about your purpose?

My Life Purpose Is:

Write your life purpose out on a 3x5 card, carry it with you and review it several times a day until you have it memorized. Feel free to amend it as you go.

Getting on Target

In order to help yourself focus on and nourish your purpose, begin by building a personal empowering target. This will provide you information about your preferred forms of personal support. (Later you will build a target for your team and congregation. With these targets you can guide, direct and monitor your individual and collective actions to fulfill your personal purpose and congregational mission.)

On your empowering target, your purpose is symbolized as the center "bulls-eye".

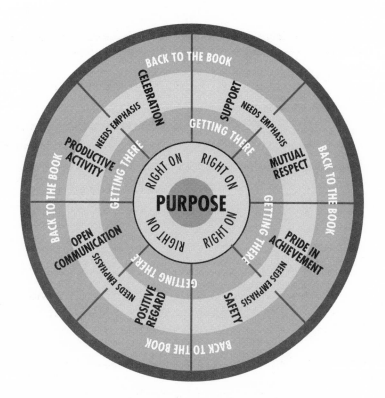

Building and using the target fulfills two of the major criteria of quality management:

1). Focus on purpose.

2). Focus on continuous improvement.

In Quality Management staying focused on these two goals has proven to increase productivity and quality outcomes in organizations. We've found that it does the same for individuals.

Your target, when completed, will have eight sections and four rings which you can use to consciously monitor and evaluate your needs and progress. By creating a personal target, you'll find that it will be easier to stay purpose-focused and improvement-oriented.

The eight sections of the Personal Empowering Target are
- Support
- Empathy
- Self Disclosure
- Safety
- Positive Connection
- Clear Communication
- Productive Activity
- Celebration

The four rings of the target indicate your percentages of success:
- 25% = needs information
- 50% = needs emphasis
- 75% = getting there
- 90 to 100% = on target

By completing the exercises, by identifying the specific acts that nourish each of these eight elements and by sharing your insights with the significant people in your network, you strengthen your skills to:

1). create positive alliances, and

2). build interpersonal bridges.

The Empowering Target Work Sheet

Instructions: On a large sheet of paper write out five actions that provide for you each of the conditions indicated in the heading,

Support/Warmth
1.
2.
3.
4.
5.

Empathy/Respect
1.
2.
3.
4.
5.

Self Discovery/Disclosure
1.
2.
3.
4.
5.

Safety
1.
2.
3.
4.
5.

Positive Regard
1.
2.
3.
4.
5.

Open Communication
1.
2.
3.
4.
5.

Productive Activity

1.
2.
3.
4.
5.

Reward/Celebration

1.
2.
3.
4.
5.

Instructions: Write your life purpose here:

Alliances with people and bridges between people are the infrastructure of empowering relationships. They are to personal empowerment what streets and highways are to transportation.

Interpersonal bridges are the adult replication of the natural cycle of attachment, bonding, separating and individuating through which human beings healthfully grow and develop. These bridges are built out of safety, positive connection, clear communication, productive activity and rewards/celebration.

Positive Alliances and Interpersonal Bridges

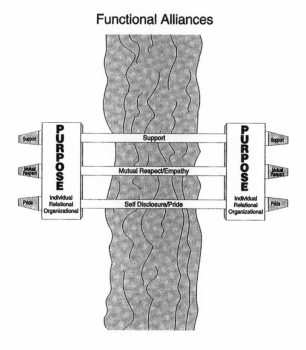

Functional Alliances

Interpersonal Bridges

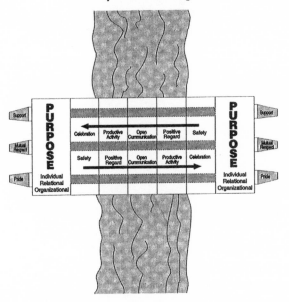

Interpersonal Bridges Exercise

Draw the target above and write your purpose in the center. In each section write five words that represent each of these conditions to you. For example – Safety: understanding, recognition, love, happiness and warmth. Once you have completed the target, say the words aloud. Be aware of how you feel when you say each word. If any of the words produce tension, replace it with a word that produces comfort. Post this target where you will see it regularly and each time you notice it, read the words aloud.

As you proceed to the exercises that follow, you will be refining the key words you have written down and want to change some of them. However, before you finally accept a word, always test it by reading it aloud. If your selected words feel comfortable, they are in resonance with your purpose – "the song in your heart." If your words cause you to feel tension or stress, they are somewhat dissonant with your purpose. Stay with the process until you have five key words that feel safe and warm.

Support

It is well-established that the single most critical factor in raising healthy children is the availability of caring in the form of
warm, nourishing caretakers. Support is to adults as "availability
of caring" is to children. Support/warmth comes in many forms
and is received as such—as phone calls, notes, touches, hugs, offers
of assistance, affirmations, appreciation and recognition—almost
any form of positive recognition.

Support is the currency of positive alliances. In the formative
years, a child's successful completion of developmental tasks is
virtually impossible without caretakers available for warmth and
instruction. However, the need for support in the form of caring
relationships does not end with biological maturation. It remains
with us throughout life.

As adults, we are fully responsible for making our own ar-
rangements for support. Because of this ever-present need, we develop friendships, organizations and community. These provide us
with human resources as we strive to detect and fulfill our purpose, but unless we use all our capacities to create supportive relationships within our organizations and communities, we are prone
to fall into ritualized niceness rather than create deep and meaningful connections. This is why we find congregations "scratching
people where they don't itch." They might offer polite acceptance
when people are coming for deep personal connections.

For the sake of simplicity, in colloquial terms, a positive alliance can be characterized as being on one's SIDE and a negative
alliance may be characterized as being on one's CASE. By arranging
with others to be on your side, you create positive alliances that
provide comfort and nourishment.

Just as knowing that someone else is on your side feels good
and allows you to venture and take chances with them, so being
on your own side feels good and encourages you to venture and
grow. By identifying the acts that support you and create warmth,

you'll be better able to stay on your own side and also be able to let others know how to support you and vice versa.

In *Able and Equal* Denton Roberts wrote the following:

The Primary Question: Am I On My Side or On My Case?

Each of us creates many words of internal dialogue (self talk) a day. These words can have negative, neutral or positive content. As we begin to notice the content of our internal dialogue, we realize that we can shape it so that it is predominantly positive, problem solving and creative, rather than negative, problem creating and destructive.

I refer to internal dialogue as either on my side (positive commentary) or on my case (negative commentary). By this I mean that we either carry on a positive and nurturing internal dialogue (on our side) or we carry on a negative and critical internal dialogue (on our case). When we're on our side we can sustain great amounts of external stress. The Jews who physically and psychologically survived the concentration camps demonstrated the extreme illustration of this ...

By regularly noticing whether we are on our side or on our case, we can increase the amount of positive support we give ourselves. With greater positive support we become aware of new options for dealing with problems, from personal to social. By choosing to be on our side we coöperate with and enhance our natural instincts to grow and develop harmoniously.

My Technique for Staying on My Side

I carry a picture of myself as a child in my wallet. It is one of those "School Days, 1941-42" pictures of a little boy I know more intimately than any other person in my life. Everywhere I go, he goes and everywhere I've been, he's been. He's always wanted people to understand him, care for him and cherish him. He's never wanted people to mistreat him. Many times he hasn't known what to do, or precisely what would satisfy him. Many times he's bubbled with enthusiasm, been consumed by curiosity, petrified with fear, overwhelmed with grief, filled with rage and warmed with love. This child that I know most intimately has been through the whole range of human experiences and wants someone to understand, appreciate and care about him at all times.

I carry his picture to remind me of his need and sensitivity. I'm the one who knows him best. I'm with him at all times and I'm the one he is most free to rely on. He depends on me to treat him well. Unless I pay attention to his feelings, unless I nurture and support him, he is in serious trouble. When I care for him properly, he will get his needs met. When his needs are met, he lives in a state of health, experiencing the world in a relaxed manner.

On the other hand, this boy whose picture I carry will become more and more desperate if I don't pay attention to his needs, wants and feelings. He will feel stress if I ignore or mistreat him over a period of time. He will resort to desperate acts for relief. In the same manner that people who are cut off from contact with others take desperate action to meet their need for human contact, so the boy in me will become desperate if I constantly ignore his needs.

Just as this boy was dependent on parents to pay attention to his feelings and to treat them properly when he was young, so too my feelings as an adult send requests for attention from me. My sense of health and well being is determined by how I respond to those messages. My choice of being on my side or on my case is critical to my sense of well being. Since I relate to myself every moment and in every situation of life, it is imperative that I recognize how I am relating to myself and that I be on my side (pp.38-39).

Exercise

Instructions: Complete the following:

Five essential qualities that create support/warmth for me are:

1.

2.

3.

4.

5.

(Read through the words you have just written, if any produce tension or stress find a replacement that produces comfort.)

Instructions:
- Reduce the essential qualities of support/warmth to five words and write them in the section on support/warmth in the target worksheet and on the large target you have created.
- Transcribe the five essential qualities of support/warmth onto a 3x5 card and carry it with you and review it several times a day.

Empathy/Mutual Respect

We all have had the experience of feeling real physical pain when we see a child get hurt and we've also been emotionally moved to profound feelings when we witness tender acts of human kindness. These feelings are based on our ability to empathize – this ability to feel for another is one of our most distinctively human characteristics. Empathy is the foundation of mutual respect. When you are on your side you experience empathy for yourself. When you are on another's side you empathize with them. In pain and pleasure, in loss and victory, empathy and mutual respect mold alliances that nourish healthful relationships.

The better you know and minister to your own and others' needs for support/warmth, the greater your respect and empathy become. In community, creating relationships that nourish and foster respect and empathy cannot be left to chance. As we consciously and effectively arrange and orchestrate mutual respect and empathy, we secure and strengthen the ties that bind us together.

Whether life is difficult or easy, troubled or running smoothly, we bond when empathy and mutual respect are abundantly available. Respect and empathy bespeak the deep connections that grow as you consciously maintain empowering relationships. By identifying how respect and empathy are best conveyed to you, by sharing this information with others, you directly support the bonding process. When empathy and mutual respect occurs between two individuals, in a group or among wide-reaching constituencies, such encounters are like that moment which the Psalmist describes: "Deep calleth unto deep" (42:7).

Robert Hill met Brent Schmitt at an organizing event for a chapter of the Disciples Peace Fellowship. There was a good dose of respect and empathy in each of them for the work the other was doing and they made a conscious effort to get to know each other better in the months that followed. Sharing their stories, they talked of similar commitments and met each other's circles of friends. In time, a solid friendship developed and the bond of their empathy and mutual respect expanded. In their personal relationship they eventually celebrated each other's weddings with great joy. Socially, they led the Disciples Peace Fellowship chapter to do some of the most innovative and creative peacemaking work in their local association of churches. Personally and socially, they could describe the development of their friendship as "deep calling unto deep."

Through the exchange of respect and empathy, alliances are systematically reinforced. The following exercise will assist you in isolating the actions that let you know respect and empathy are available to you.

Exercise

Instructions: Complete the following:

My most memorable experiences of empathy and mutual respect were:

1.

2.

3.

4.

5.

Reflecting on the above experiences of empathy and mutual respect, how do others communicate to you their empathy and mutual respect?

1.

2.

3.

4.

5.

How do you communicate empathy to yourself?

Instructions: Extrapolating from the above exercise, create a list of five words that describe empathy/respect for you and then write them in your EMPOWERING TARGET worksheet and on your large target.

1.

2.

3.

4.

5.

(Read through the words you have just written, if any produce tension or stress find a replacement that produces comfort.)

Self-Discovery/Disclosure

As we invite others into our lives, we disclose ourselves; and as others disclose themselves to us, they invite us into their lives. The third dimension of positive alliances is self-discovery and disclosure—which go hand in hand with each other. Through disclosure we discover and with discovery we disclose. As we disclose our discoveries about our selves, our lives and our faith with one another, we deepen our interdependence.

Disclosure leads to discovery and discovery leads to disclosure. It's a synergistic process. More than likely, we have experienced this synergy most profoundly in past spiritual and intimate experiences. Through the synergy of disclosure and discovery, our identity is enhanced, our competency is expanded, our self-esteem grows and we develop healthful pride.

In our early developing years outside recognition of our uniqueness builds our self-esteem and our sense of competency. As children we built things, brought home papers, etc. When these achievements were adequately recognized, we naturally felt pride and our sense of self-worth and competency was built. Throughout our lives, beyond the early developmental years, we need ways to recognize and validate our own uniqueness.

It was Abraham Maslow who first recognized a human paradox. He noted there was a certain amount of each human being that was actualized and a certain amount that was potential. This was not new, but what was new was that Maslow observed that each time people actualized some of their potential they discovered their potential was greater than originally thought. He used the analogy of an iceberg: 90% is below the water and 10% is above the water. Each time you shave off the ten percent above the water, it produces a larger mass above the water. So the paradox is we constantly discover how great our potential is as we actualize it. This is called self-actualization. It is fair to conclude that our potential at any time is greater than what we currently recognize.

The disclosing of our self leads to discovery of our capacities and discovery culminates in healthful pride. Pride is an "accompanying phenomenon" – it comes along with something we do or some way we are being. Since we are developing throughout every stage of life, learning to foster and reinforce our own and others' healthy pride is critical to our ongoing development – or our self-actualizing.

In the Christian tradition, we may say that this was Jesus' challenge to Nathaniel at the time he called him to become his disciple: "You will see greater things than these" (Jn 1:50). The interplay of self-discovery and disclosure is also at the heart of Jesus' challenge to the entire group of his initial followers: "Very truly, I tell you, the one who believes in me will also do the works that I do and, in fact, will do greater works than these" (Jn 14:12).

In quality management theory one of the major insights that lead to success is to "remove barriers to pride." We take this a step further and suggest that empowering processes regularly recognize, encourage and reinforce self-discovery and disclosure which often culminates in pride.

Exercise

Instructions: Complete the following:

1. The ways I recognize and share my achievements are:

2. The ways I like to be recognized as capable and competent by others are:

3. In order to disclose myself and foster pride in achievement I need:

Instructions: Condense to five words the kinds of recognition you like for achievement and add to your empowering Target Worksheet.
(Read through the words you have just written, if any produce tension or stress find a replacement that produces comfort.)

What Happened to Bill, Sue, Ted, Sally and Fred?

Back at the Ranch with Bill Emp ...

After Bill and the team identified their purpose and began to make explicit the types of support/warmth, empathy/respect and discovery/disclosure they personally needed, they experienced a deepening of the bonds between themselves. When differences of opinion came up they found that it was easier to understand where the other was coming from – and they also looked forward to their meetings.

Their tasks seemed less burdensome and as they identified problems in the congregation they were not as easily perplexed or discouraged. When they had to deal with unhappy congregants and difficult issues they were able to look beyond the "problem" and see the issue of concern that caused the problem. By strengthening their own alliances with each other they were better prepared to develop strategies to strengthen alliances within the congregation.

Conclusion

You have now completed the three conditions – warmth/support, empathy/respect and self-discovery/disclosure – that establish healthful alliances. When you have positive alliances you have safety. Safety is the first step in building interpersonal bridges. Interpersonal bridges connect you with others so you can exchange life-enhancing commodities freely.

Think for a moment of how it would be if you knew the preferred forms for establishing positive alliances for each of your congregants.

From Positive Alliances to Interpersonal Bridges

Positive alliances make possible the building of Interpersonal Bridges. Interpersonal Bridges provide the pathways and networks through which we exchange energy, solve problems and renew our vitality. Community comes into being when strong interpersonal bridges abound.

When Temple Beth Shalom created a "Father Family Fun Night" program, several younger fathers in the congregation formed some mutually invigorating positive alliances among a growing number in their group. During fellowship times after worship, over lunch and then in the Brotherhood Steering Committee, the younger fathers discovered the beginnings of a very powerful empowering format. Through the interplay of self-discovery and disclosure, bonds of mutual support and warm empathy and respect were formed.

Subsequently the younger fathers decided to invite all of Beth Shalom's fathers to enjoy a monthly get-together they would call "Father Family Fun Night." With fathers and their children gathering in the comfortable confines of Beth Shalom's social hall, with kid-friendly food and with videos and simple games available, the stage was set for the building of interpersonal bridges. Over the months and years, these young fathers became buddies who supported each other in tribulation and loss, in joy and in sorrow. (A "bonus bridge" was also experienced by the younger mothers who enjoyed a "night off" each month. When interpersonal bridges are created, everybody wins!)

Interpersonal bridges create an empowering cycle. An empowering cycle in a relationship is an adult replication of the natural developmental cycle of attachment, bonding, separating and individuating. The Empowering Cycle (safety, positive connections, open communication, productive activity and rewards/celebration). outlines the essential elements necessary to establish, build and maintain interpersonal bridges.

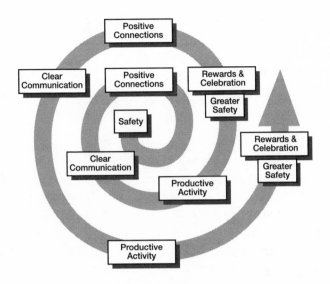

For individuals to maintain empowering relationships it is most helpful to be able to articulate explicitly what nourishes each of the dimensions of the empowering cycle. When we have identified the actions that empower us, we:

- recognize empowering actions when they occur;

- arrange relationships so that they provide nurturance; and

- inform and invite others to assist us in our pursuit of fulfilling our purpose.

As individuals within a group (such as a board or committee) know and share empowering actions, they provide each other explicit information that strengthens a sense of community. Further, when groups identify actions that empower and use them to guide their interactions, they create an empowering ethos—a healthy community.

How the Empowering Process Works

In *The Road Ahead*, Bill Gates states that businesses operate in positive and negative spirals. In positive spirals, creativity, investment and personnel are attracted. In negative spirals, creativity is discouraged, investors are wary and the best personnel leave. This phenomenon is also true for institutions. Empowering occurs naturally in a cycle in which one thing builds on another in a logical sequence.

In other words, empowering begins with Safety. Safety leads to Positive Connection. Positive Connection leads to Open Communication. Open Communication leads to Productive Activity. And Productive Activity leads to Rewards and Celebration. Rewards and Celebration complete the cycle and in turn nourish purpose and expand our base of safety.

The Empowering Cycle can occur in a brief conversation with a friend, in a short-term project at work, in a long-term project like raising children and over the course of a lifetime, like fulfilling our purpose. The better we understand the process, the better we know what to do to advance it in the here and now.

As you think through what empowers you, you'll recognize that acceptance, understanding, praise, inclusion and realistic expectations are empowering actions. Conversely, blame, ridicule, humiliation, alienation and unrealistic expectations are dis-empowering actions. Ironically, the very actions that dis-empower are frequently touted as empowering and are often used by many to motivate when difficulties arise. The actions that empower, on the other hand, are frequently only used after a successful achievement. Seldom are they used when we are encountering difficulties. In our culture it is not unusual to criticize failure when what we really need to do is to praise effort. In so doing we dis-empower rather than empower.

Both our general culture and our individual training encourage

Empowering Congregations

us to use subtle forms of blame, ridicule, humiliation, alienation and unrealistic expectations when we are encountering difficulties in life. We are prone to use dis-empowering actions when we need to be empowered. Frequently when we have a failure the first thing we look for is fault – who can I blame? "It's your own fault" is seldom a helpful piece of information.

Using dis-empowering actions creates a self-defeating situation by perpetuating a reign of error if not terror. Without careful attention to empowering, we blame when we need to praise, we ridicule when we need to understand, we humiliate when we need to accept, we alienate when we need to include and we set unrealistic expectations when we need to set realistic expectations. (As we state in workshops: "If criticism were healing, the whole world would be well.")

To establish empowering processes in yourself and your organizations, you need an understanding of the logical progression by which empowering occurs and is sustained. The Empowering Cycle provides you with a model. It also serves as a tool with which to identify what to emphasize when empowering is not occurring.

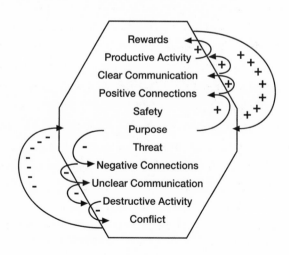

Positive Spiral
(Empowering)

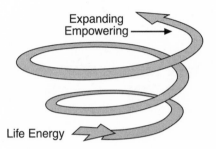

Expanding
Empowering

Life Energy

The Components and Progression of the Empowering Cycle

- Safety

- Positive Connections

- Open Communication

- Productive Activity

- Rewards/Celebration

The empowering cycle is nourished by:

- understanding

- acceptance

- praise

- inclusion

- realistic expectations

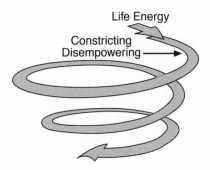

Negative Spiral
(Disempowering)

Life Energy

Constricting
Disempowering

The Dis-empowering Cycle

Just as there is a cycle that is empowering, so there is a cycle that is dis-empowering. The empowering cycle builds community and the dis-empowering cycle destroys community. The dis-empowering cycle is energized by certain acts. These too we must understand fully to pursue optimal functioning. The following is the dysfunctional empowering cycle.

Components and Progression of the Dis-empowerment Cycle

- Danger/Threat

- Negative Regard

- Closed Communication

- Destructive Activity

- Conflict/ Hassles/Violence

The dis-empowering cycle is energized by:

- blame

- ridicule

- humiliation

- unrealistic expectations

- alienation

The Empowering Cycle, when reinforced regularly, builds interpersonal bridges and the Dis-empowering Cycle, when reinforced regularly, erodes interpersonal bridges.

The Empowering and Disempowering Cycles in Action

When we first shared the empowering and dis-empowering cycles with a manager of a company, he commented, "But the dis-empowering cycle is so easy!" Indeed, we easily slip into the dis-empowering cycle. Most of us have been well schooled in the actions of the dis-empowering cycle. Therefore, keeping our energies in the empowering cycle is often difficult.

Like the exercise of folding your hands with the other thumb on top, staying in the empowering process takes conscious attention. In order to create empowering connections with self and others you need first to develop a consciousness of and a familiarity with the empowering process. In the following section, Interpersonal Bridges, you will isolate the ways your empowering is energized.

COMPONENTS AND PROGRESSION
EMPOWERING CYCLE

Nourished by: praise, understanding, acceptance,
realistic performance expectations, and incorporation

****

SAFETY
Outcome :
ESTABLISHMENT OF SELF
PROVIDES IDENTITY AND LEADS TO ATTACHMENT

POSITIVE RELATIONS
Outcome :
ATTACHMENT AND BONDING OF SELF TO PEOPLE AND GOALS
CREATES BONDING AND LEADS TO ENGAGEMENT

OPEN COMMUNICATION
Outcome :
ENGAGEMENT OF SELF WITH OTHERS AND THE ENVIRONMENT
STRENGTHENS BONDING THROUGH ENGAGEMENT
AND BEGINS INDIVIDUATION

PRODUCTIVE / EFFECTIVE ACTION
Outcome :
ACTUALIZATION THAT LEADS TO FULFILLMENT
STIMULATES CREATIVITY AND LEADS TO INCORPORATION

CELEBRATION
Outcome :
INCORPORATION THAT BUILDS EMOTIONAL SAFETY
PROVIDES INTIMACY, ATTACHMENT AND REINFORCES
THE ESTABLISHMENT OF SELF AT DEEPER LEVEL
****

COMPONENTS AND PROGRESSION
DIS-EMPOWERING CYCLE
*Nourished by: blame ridicule, humiliation, unrealistic performance
expectations, and alienation
****

DANGER / THREAT
Outcome :
DIS-ESTABLISHMENT OF SELF
THREATENS IDENTITY AND LEADS TO DETACHMENT FROM PEOPLE AND GOALS

NEGATIVE RELATIONS
Outcome :
DETACHMENT ISOLATION
REINFORCES DETACHMENT AND LEADS TO ISOLATION

UNCLEAR OR CLOSED COMMUNICATION
Outcome :
DISENGAGEMENT WITH OTHERS
REINFORCES ISOLATION AND LEADS TO ALIENATION

UNPRODUCTIVE / DESTRUCTIVE ACTIVITY
Outcome :
ALIENATES AND ISOLATES SELF AND OTHERS
PROVIDES FALSE SENSE OF SAFETY AND POWER

CONFUSION / CONFLICT / VIOLENCE
Outcome :
DESTRUCTION OF SELF
VENTILATES PAIN AND HEIGHTENS ISOLATION AND INTENSIFIES DANGER

Interpersonal Bridges

- Safety

- Positive Connect Ions

- Open Communication

- Productive Activity

- Rewards and Celebration

Chapter 4

Building Interpersonal Bridges

In human systems dependable interpersonal bridges are established on safety–physical, emotional, intellectual and spiritual. When safety exists in interpersonal relations we have a secure base. With a secure base we are free to explore, learn and discover–as a well-nurtured child is free to explore, learn and discover. Without a secure base we are guarded and do not feel free to contribute and explore.

Interpersonal bridges are built by mutual agreements between people, implicit and/or explicit, to be resources to one another–to "be there for" each other–to be on each other's "side." At times the bridges that connect us are called on to bear physical loads, at times spiritual and at times emotional. Much of the time all three areas are in demand.

The prototypes for building such bridges are found in families. Functional families provide members adequate support, guidance and encouragement – secure bases. Interpersonal bridges provide the same secure base for adults and create community. Specific information about your own and others' safety-needs helps you intentionally establish dependable and serviceable interpersonal bridges.

As said earlier, being skilled at creating interpersonal bridges requires the same in-depth concentration, discipline and knowledge of human functioning that a professional musician or athlete uses regarding their music or sport. And as athletes and musicians hone their skills by mastering each dimension in their field of endeavor step-by-step, so we develop well-honed skills by building interpersonal bridges.

The components of interpersonal bridges build upon each other in a cyclical fashion. Each piece provides the foundation for the next. In an empowering cycle we naturally move from safety to positive connections, to open communication, to productive activity, to rewards / celebration.

Review in your mind a successful problem-solving experience you have recently had and you will see how all the elements of the empowering cycle were present. The following section will help you begin the process of developing your "professional" skills for creating and maintaining interpersonal bridges.

Safety

Safety is a feeling that is created in the context of your environment. Each of us has specific requirements for safety. When these requirements are met we are free to venture, create and explore. When they are not met you don't feel free to venture. The better you understand your own and others' safety requirements the easier it is to develop and maintain environments that feel safe.

The four primary dimensions to safety in any relationship are: physical, intellectual, emotional and spiritual. Security in these aspects of our lives is as essential for intellectual, emotional and spiritual growth as food is for physical growth.

Bill, Sue Ted, Sally and Fred's Experience

When Bill first thought about safety as essential to empowering, he thought that it was too simple and self-evident. "Everyone knows that!" he mused. The others felt the same way, but what Bill discovered when he'd been concentrating on empowering and flow was that being aware of his degree of safety was very closely related to his sense of well-being and performance.

As he isolated what made him feel safe physically, intellectually, emotionally and spiritually he discovered he had varying levels of safety through the course of the day. When presenting new ideas, he often didn't feel very safe. Performing routine tasks he felt very safe. When confronting new situations he sometimes felt slight apprehension. By assessing his degree of safety and making sure he had access to things that provided safety, Bill found it helped him determine what to do, how much to venture and when to back off.

When Bill introduced safety to his team he told them that at first he thought it was silly to point out something as simple and self-evident as safety, but he had learned that paying direct attention to his feelings of safety was critical to his effectiveness and his degree of flow.

Bill also remembered an experience they had shared a few years before when a certain trustee had been in charge of doing the payroll for the staff of First Church. For whatever reason – comical or power-tripping – this trustee was often heard walking the halls of the church and muttering within earshot of the staff a mournful refrain: "I know payroll is due pretty soon, but I sure hope we have a good offering this coming Sunday, 'cause I'm not sure if we can pay everybody." (The trustee said this despite the fact that a payday had never been missed nor even late once.)

Bill recalled how he had decided to establish a policy of safety with the next trustee charged with the payroll responsibilities: The dependability of payday was to be maintained with consistency and gladness. "I didn't express it in these terms at the time, but we were helping create an environment of safety," Bill remembered.

The others also recalled the change in the staff morale after that policy was instituted and agreed it was a lot more secure (and fun) for the staff (and the church as a whole) to function in a situation of safety. Bill wondered what would have happened if he had confronted the trustee and set about creating an environment of safety back then. "Maybe I could have if we had been using this process." Sally responded, "And it could have saved a lot of emotional and spiritual wear-and-tear on our staff ! Maybe it even would have been instructive and helpful for the trustee."

After Ted, Sally, Sue and Fred created their maps and targets, they shared with the others their experience. Sue said it best, "I've discovered that even grown-ups need to pay attention to safety." All five acknowledged that knowing what made the others feel safe made their work together much easier.

The following exercise will help you begin to delineate your personal criterion for safety.

Exercise

Instructions: Think of yourself and the people with whom you are deeply attached. Envision yourself with them and answer the following questions:

Physical safety for me has the following characteristics:

1.

2.

3.

4.

5.

I feel most physically safe when:

1.

2.

3.

4.

5.

Reflecting on the above information, what do you need to maintain physical safety?

Intellectual safety for me has the following characteristics:

1.

2.

3.

4.

5.

I feel most intellectually safe when:

1.

2.

3.

4.

5.

Reflecting on the above, what do I need in order to maintain intellectual safety?

Emotional safety for me has the following characteristics:

1.

2.

3.

4.

5.

I feel most emotionally safe when:

1.

2.

3.

4.

5.

Reflecting on the above, what do I need to maintain emotional safety?

Spiritual safety for me has the following characteristics:

1.

2.

3.

4.

5.

I feel most spiritually safe when:

1.

2.

3.

4.

5.

Reflecting on the above, what do I need to maintain spiritual safety.

> Instructions: Read through the words, if any produce tension or stress find a word to replace it that produces comfort. Condense and add it to your empowering target worksheet in the section on safety.

Positive Connection

Positive connections are the lubricant of relationships – they reinforce safety and allow relationships to grow. When we are positively connected we are glad to see one another, we feel free to share our thoughts and goals, we are willing to ask for help and we are eager for new adventures. Conversely, when we do not feel positively connected we are guarded and isolated.

Bill and the Team's Experience with Positive Connections

Bill's insight that safety paves the way for positive connections was remarkably simple. Yet what he experienced was that when he knew he was safe he was free to look about him for what he liked. He remembered reading that the freedom of focus was one of the unsung freedoms we human beings have. Feeling safe allowed him to look for what he could positively connect with in nature, in his relationships and in life as a whole.

As Bill developed his "flow" experiment he isolated the actions that reinforced his positive connections. Reminding himself of his personal criteria for positive connections helped him to recognize when he was positively connected and prodded him to arrange for positive connections when he felt the need of support.

When Bill told his team about this discovery, they at first seemed equally skeptical of such a simple process. Yet, as they did the exercises they found that their experience was similar to Bill's. Like safety, positive connections were so basic they were often overlooked.

Sue brought up an inspiring event in the life of First Church that seemed to give a vivid word-picture to the notion of positive connection. "Remember what happened with Brian and Kirk?" she asked. These two had seemingly been the least likely people ever to make connection, positive or negative, of any kind.

Kirk was 50, an elder, a former moderator of the church's board, an African-American and a leader in his auto-workers' union. He gave steadfast, quiet guidance to the congregation and was well-known and much beloved by the First Church family.

On the other hand Brian was a poor, white 14-year-old kid from the so-called "wrong-side-of-the-tracks." He rarely appeared to have much energy and always looked like he was having a bad day. It only took a brief conversation with Brian for most folks to discern Brian had a ways to go before he felt good about himself and the world around him.

Somehow Brian and Kirk took a liking to each other and despite their great differences, felt safe enough to make positive connections with each other. Brian helped Kirk with the bus run to pick up folks for church. They regularly sat with each other in worship and Brian took particular pleasure and pride passing the communion trays each week to Kirk and to those down his aisle. Before long Brian had a noticeable "spring in his step" and smiled a lot more. Life began to appear enjoyable for him. In fact, to all

Empowering Congregations

those who knew the "old Brian" he seemed to have experienced a complete transformation. These positive connections with Kirk had obviously made a great difference for him.

"I remember how you described it in a retreat meditation a while back, Bill," Sue recalled. "You said, Brian knows he's still poor and he knows he's still white, but he also knows he's not trash anymore.' Wow!" The group concluded that making positive connections was indeed an empowering experience.

Exercises

Instructions: Complete

- The most effective form of positive strokes for me is ...

- Analyzing the above information I need to be in situations where there is an abundance of ...

(Read through the words you have just written, if any produce tension or stress find a replacement that produces comfort. Condense to five key words and add to your Empowering Target.)

Open Communication

Open communication naturally follows safety and positive connection. When we feel safe and are well connected we tell each other about our world, life, perceptions, confusions, problems, goals and aspirations. Once we have safety on our four levels of experience (physical, intellectual, spiritual and emotional) and we connect positively with one another, we naturally venture into new areas, explore our curiosity and discover new dimensions of life through communication.

Setting the stage for the free flow of communication has both general and specific requirements. Generally we need an environment free of the shaming, threats of blame, ridicule, humiliation, unrealistic expectations or alienation. Specifically we need an environment where there is an abundance of acceptance, understanding, praise, realistic expectations and inclusion.

To put it in summary fashion: Open communication flourishes in the presence of acceptance, understanding, praise, inclusion and realistic expectation and open communication withers in the presence of blame, ridicule, humiliation, alienation and unrealistic expectations.

Bill and the Team's Experience with Open Communication

Bill learned from his research that communication is the most frequently identified culprit when human systems malfunction. It doesn't seem to matter whether the experts are describing parenting or organizational development, whether they are addressing issues of international relations or the difficulty children have in school: communication, or the lack thereof, is most frequently identified as the source of interpersonal problems.

Bill had extensive experience as a leader and counselor working with congregations, committees, individuals, couples and families. He realized there are so many different styles of communication, interpretations of meaning and inference that it was easy to see why communication was the most frequently identified human problem. But he also knew that when safety and positive connections were present, people were able to communicate even on the most difficult topics. He had always worked to get people well connected rather than convert them to a particular style of communication.

Bill presented this next step in the empowering cycle to his team by telling them that since communication problems were so complex and difficult to isolate, he had found that concentrating on maintaining the conditions necessary for open communication was the key. Thus he told Ted, Fred, Sue and Sally that when understanding, acceptance, praise, inclusion and realistic expectations were present communication flourished; conversely when blame, ridicule, humiliation, alienation and unrealistic expectations were present communication deteriorated.

Bill suggested to the group that they had probably been practicing open communication for at least a year before they formed themselves into a group. "Do you remember when we were having a bit of trouble starting up new programs? We were feeling safe enough and positive connections were being established, but we seemed to be misfiring when it came to understanding, acceptance, inclusion and having realistic expectations. I'll never forget how Lily helped straighten us out at that board meeting when she proposed the rule of thumb we now operate on. I've memorized her suggestion: 'Let us affirm that you can do anything once at First Church. If it doesn't work, then please don't ever do it again. If it does work, then please do it again, only not next week. We want to keep things lively.' I'd call that pretty open communication." They all nodded in agreement.

The following exercises will guide you in this process.

Exercise

Instructions: Complete

● When I feel blamed, ridiculed, humiliated, unrealistic expectations or alienated I ...

● When I feel praised, accepted, understood and when I experience realistic expectations and inclusion, I ...

Add the words "praise, understanding, acceptance, inclusion and realistic expectations" to your target in the section "Open communication." Beside these words write your own words. Be sure to read through the words, if any produce tension or stress find a word to replace it that produces comfort.

PRODUCTIVE ACTIVITY

Productive activity is fulfilling purpose. "If you live yard-by-yard, life sure is hard. If you live life inch-by-inch, life's a cinch" – Rosa Parks' mother.

Open communication provides new information, insight, resources and experience. When acted upon, open communication regularly leads to productive activity. Successful productive activity builds confidence, establishes competence and strengthens self-esteem. With each productive activity the fulfillment of purpose and mission becomes increasingly possible.

Productive activity ranges from developing a deeper spiritual life to solving institutional problems, from creating space capsules to consoling a friend in grief. It can be as simple as maintaining environments that are compatible with our tastes, as delicate as resolving personality differences, or as complex as instilling values in our children.

Bill and the Team's Experience with Productive Activity

As Bill and his team developed their own empowering processes they became aware of each other's empowering preferences. It's not surprising that they also became more productive and fulfilled. With safety, positive connections and open communication in the forefront of their minds, they found it was easier to reach consensus and perform their assigned duties. Fred claimed it was easier to prepare and present his financial reports because he knew they would be welcomed and appreciated. "If it's bad news, I know you guys are going to help me deal with it and if its good news, I know it's going to make you happy. Funny what this empowering stuff does."

Although Bill originally feared introducing the cycle he'd developed – thinking it might be shot down because it was so simple – he began to see it was creating more profound effects than he'd originally hoped for. Besides, all the dimensions of his work were increasingly meaningful and rewarding and he was spending more and more time in flow.

Bill, Sue, Sally, Ted and Fred all agreed "this empowering stuff" had proved beneficial to each of them and to the congregation as a whole. They each made a commitment to bring up the "empowering cycle," particularly its focus on productive activity, the next time they were part of any long-range or planning-team meetings for First Church. Ted said it for all of them: "Can you imagine what we might be able to accomplish in the next five years, if we instituted the 'empowering cycle' across the broad range of our congregation's current projects and future dreams?"

Exercise

Instructions: Complete the following

● In order for me to feel that an activity is productive, it has to meet the following criteria:

● Past activities that met my criteria were:

● From the above lists I conclude:

Reduce your criteria for productive activity to five key words and write them on your target. Read through the words, if any produce tension or stress, find a word to replace it that produces comfort.

Rewards / Celebration

Rewards and Celebration complete the cycle of empowering. When we are rewarded and when we celebrate, we recognize our achievements, revitalize ourselves and reinforce our successes; therefore we expand our base of safety as, inch-by-inch, we discern and fulfill our purpose.

Rewards / Celebration naturally flow with successful productive activity. They renew and expand our esteem for others and ourselves. Through rewarding and celebrating a personal achievement, an organizational milestone or significant life event, we finalize it. As we bring the achievements, milestones and events of our lives to closure through celebration, they become a part of our self-image and expand our esteem. Nothing succeeds like success.

We've been pastors of congregations that celebrated their attainments and achievements with flair and flourish. Whether it was a particular congregant's milestone of 50 years of membership or a special wedding anniversary or a successful capital campaign or a child's birth or building a Habitat for Humanity house or a Sunday school class teacher's years of continuous service, celebration has been a key "punctuation point" in the churches we have served. And in each celebration, there is an impetus for further achievement and attainment, a further point of inspiration for working out our faith commitments.

Personal achievements, milestones and significant events left un-celebrated remain open and incomplete. When this is the case, we may end up feeling that what we achieved wasn't worth our effort and therefore we may not be re-energized for the next step on our journey. We may even slip into a negative spiral. Rewards and celebration revitalize us and keep us in a positive spiral as we move step-by-step to fulfill our personal and congregational mission. Each successful movement through the entire empowering cycle can be compared to a graduation of sorts – it affirms our competency, stimulates creativity and expands our horizons.

Bill and the Team's Experience with Rewards and Celebration

At the annual ice cream social, Bill decided to add an awards celebration to the festivities. "Everybody will be enjoying all those great deserts and having a good time. It will be just the right moment to mark some great successes, individually and group-wise, in the congregation," Bill reasoned.

After all the ice cream had been dipped and the cakes and cookies had been delighted in, about two dozen awards were given out for distinctive achievements by First Church members. Bill had contacted the various committees in the congregation and group leaders for suggestions. The atmosphere in the church's fellowship hall became charged with excitement and satisfaction as awards were given out for deacon service (The "Hello-I'll-Be-Your-Server-Today" Award), teaching excellence (The "Light of Knowledge" Award), evangelism efforts (The "Each-One-Bring-One" Award), special volunteer efforts (The "Second Mile" Award), janitorial assistance (The "Cleanliness-Is-Next-to-Godliness" Award), leadership in the youth group (The "Future-of-the-Church" Award) and more.

"Wow," several people echoed, "We've got quite a church here, don't we? Look what all of our folks have done! This is fun! We ought to do this again next year!" With recognition and celebration enacted in the midst of the congregation, the First Church family experienced a warm glow of satisfaction and the thrill of joy. And they felt ready for whatever came next.

Bill realized the work they were about in the congregation was based on the loftiest of goals. Each person involved was attached to the congregation because they held a common vision and faith. They called it "the rule of love" and every evidence they saw of its existence gave them reason to rejoice and be encouraged. But he also realized these noble goals had been in the mind of humankind in some form or another since the beginning of time.

Fulfilling their faith was a monumental task for individuals and congregations and both needed constant inspiration and encouragement. From First Church's food pantry to their participation in the neighborhood association, their art gallery; their youth mission trips; their special carol fest at Christmas time; their ice cream social awards party; their homecoming Sunday recognition; their women's fellowship bazaar; their Serenity Sunday services sponsored by their substance abuse council; their interracial family circle; their advent service of remembrance and hope for those who have lost loved ones; their annual Martin Luther King Holiday observance; from all of these it was clear to Bill, Ted, Sally, Fred and Sue: celebration was and would remain absolutely key for the vitality and growth of First Church's family of faith.

In many ways, in both their private devotional experiences and in their shared congregational life, the leaders and the congregation celebrated. Many tangible and intangible rewards came their way as they "kept the faith." But as Bill was deciphering the empowering process he identified some subtleties he had not previously recognized. First and most important was that each time a success was celebrated they were all energized. Second, if successes were left un-rewarded or un-celebrated no one experienced this re-energizing.

Bill concluded the whole empowering cycle rested on rewards and celebration. Each time the cycle was completed, the whole congregation felt empowered. Not only did their energies go up, but their capacities and ambitions were expanded. It seemed to Bill that the more they rewarded and celebrated, the more they expanded their capacities.

"Knowing precisely what each of us considers a reward and how we like to celebrate and keeping this information in mind, we will open doors to unlimited capacities. Life is meant to be celebrated," was Bill's conclusion to the team.

Exercise

List five significant celebrations you have experienced:

1.

2.

3.

4.

5.

Recall how you felt after each celebration:

1.

2.

3.

4.

5.

List five achievements you failed to celebrate:

1.

2.

3.

4.

5.

List how you felt following those events:

1.

2.

3.

4.

5.

What conclusions do you draw from the information above?

Instructions: Create five key words that stand for celebration and add
these to the Empowering Target Worksheet.

You now have completed your personal empowering target. Create a form using the target below as a model and keep it before you. To reinforce what you have learned, discuss with trusted friends, what you have discovered.

Building Your Personal Empowering Map

Following is an outline of the Empowering Map. Copy this into your notebook with separate pages for each item.

Empowering Map Form

- My overall life purpose is ...

- My purpose right now is ...

- My overall life purpose and my current purpose relate in the following ways: (list at least five)

- To accomplish my purpose I need empowering relationships with ... (list five people)

- I am empowered by the following supportive actions: (list five)

- I experience mutual respect in the following forms: (list five)

- I feel proud when I and others ... (list five)

- I feel safe when ... (list five)

- I feel positive connection when ... (list five)

- I know communication is open when ... (list five)

- I know my activity is productive when ... (list five)

- Rewards that inspire and challenge me are ... (list five)

Empowering Plan

Once you have completed all the items, review each one again, reading your answer aloud. Be aware of your bodily experience as you do so. If you feel comfortable, leave the words as is. If you feel tension, change the words. Read aloud again and repeat this process until each of your words produces comfort when you repeat it. It may take some time and work until you get the exact words that produce comfort. Take your time.

You now have created a working map which informs you of your purpose as you currently understand it and of the actions that empower you. You can also use your map to let others know what empowers you. Sharing is sometimes risky. Before you feel safe enough to share, you may need to focus on empowering yourself in solitude. By using your target and daily worksheet to monitor yourself you have a private way to begin this process. As time goes on you may naturally want to share.

To utilize these tools effectively you will also need a plan. Here is a model you can use as a guide in making your own. Your plan must be "doable" – live life inch-by-inch, not yard-by-yard. One of the main ways we sabotage empowerment is by setting unrealistic expectations. If you find that you are not following your plan, modify it so that it realistically fits your life.

Model Plan

1. Do something small every day to define and pursue my purpose. (Keep it small. If you improve one-tenth of one-percent a day you will have improved 36.5% in a year.)

2. Share my Empowering Map with people who are important to me. (Good companions are our most important source of support and nourishment.)

3. Keep my target before me and rate myself daily. (Repetition, repetition, repetition – establishing new habits is a lot easier than breaking old habits.)

Team Training

Chapter 5

From Empowering Self to Empowering Others

Now that you have experienced and experimented with the empowering process you should be able to envision the benefit of having empowering targets, maps and plans throughout the congregation. The problem is how to get there from here. In this section you will be guided in a process to introduce this information to a team and develop a collaborative process by which you and the team can introduce these concepts to the congregation.

As you proceed you will need to tailor these processes to fit your situation. Feel free to do so. However, while there is nothing sacrosanct about the order you follow, we do believe that all the steps of the process are essential to success.

Training

The first step is to lead a team through the same material you have just been through. It is best to start with a small group of interested and like-minded colleagues – four is optimum. It is fair to assume that they may not be as motivated as you and therefore it is best to introduce them to the material in personal terms and incrementally, discussing it as you go.

We have prepared four working agendas to assist you. When this process is completed you each will have personal Empowering Targets and Maps and you will have developed a team Target.

Training Agendas

This process can be done in a series of meetings or in a retreat setting.

Preparation: Recruit your network. Introduce the process by having the participants take the self assessment you took at the beginning of the book. Give them a copy of the Bill Emp Tale and explain why you would like them to participate with you in these sessions.

Step 1 – Compile four packets from the text.
Packet #1 – pp. 1-10 & 38-41 (pass this packet out when the team participants are recruited.
Packet #2 – pp. 35-55 (to be used in session 1).
Packet #3 – pp. 56-64 (to be used in session 2).
Packet #4 – pp. 74-90 (to be used in session 3).

Session One

I. Tell your story: (30 minute max)
A. How you came to the material ...
B. What your resistances were/are ...
C. What insights you have gained thus far.
D. What you would like to see happen in the congregation.
E. Open yourself to personal questions

Step Two: In your own words, review the material on purpose. Give each person a copy of packet #2 (pp. 35-55) and let them look through them.

Step Three: Discuss the material and complete the exercises.

Session Two

Preparation: Review your workbook pages on alliances (pp. 56-64) and make notes about the positive gains you've experienced since working with these concepts. Prepare yourself to present the materials.

Step One: Ask each person to share any positive gains they had completing the section on purpose.

Step Two: Discuss how these ideas and insights might be applicable to the congregation. (Note: make notes on this session but do not make agreements for implementation at this point. You will do this together later and you all will have had time to integrate the material by then.)

Step Three: Report the positive personal gains you've had as a result of doing the exercises on alliances.

Step Four: Pass out packet #3 (pp. 55-64) – Functional Alliances

Step Five: Complete the exercises

Session Three

Preparation: Review text pages (pp. 74-90) on interpersonal bridges and make notes for presenting the material.

Step One: Share your positive experiences with the material on interpersonal bridges.

Step Two: Discuss how these concepts might be applicable to the congregation – take notes but put off making agreements for implementation.

Step Three: Pass out and work through packet #4 (pp. 74-90) — pages on interpersonal bridges.

Step Four: Complete and discuss.

Session Four

In this session you will build a Team Target by combining the targets of the members of the team. This will equip you to build the congregational target in the next session. Uyse the Target graphic on p. 90 as your model. On a large sheet of newsprint duplicate the Target before the session. Together you will mutually decide on the words to inscribe on each page. For a detailed process, use pp. 107 & 108 as a guide.

Once you have compiled your team target, discuss how this might best be introduced to the congregation.

Developing Your Congregation

Chapter 6

Developing Your Congregational Target

After developing their personal and team empowering process, Bill and the team knew that they were on to something. The focus on empowering not only kept their work together fluid and flowing, it also affected their whole lives. Now they wondered, how can we spread this through the congregation?

Sally suggested they review what they had been through and brainstorm about ways to introduce these concepts to their congregation. Fred said he thought that they should go easy with it, reminding them he had found the ideas a little "far out" when Bill first introduced them. Ted felt whatever they did should be thoroughly understood and sanctioned by the board. Sue said she had been thinking about how to use the information with the committees and had developed a form she was planning to discuss with the committee chairs. Sally said she had been discussing the material with her close friends in the congregation and they were very interested.

All agreed the way they had gradually added the "empowering dimension" to their regular routine seemed to be a good model. They developed the following plan.

The Empowering Plan

• Bill would write up how he had come to the empowering process and they would distribute his tale in the church newsletter.

- Each of them would prepare their personal reflections on how the process had affected them and their committee work in article form for the church newsletter.

- Sally would present her form to the committee chair persons at the next meeting and get their questions and responses.

- Fred and Ted would work with Bill to develop a plan for congregational implementation to present to the board.

- Bill would devote his regular column in the church newsletter to different dimensions of empowering purpose, the empowering cycle.

- As a team they would create an outline for a congregational empowering manual they would like to see implemented in the congregation.

- Sue would develop an outline for a workbook individuals could use to develop their personal empowering manuals and which would be designed to relate their personal fulfillment with the goals of the congregations.

- Bill wrote Bill Emp's Empowering Tale.

- Sally, Fred, Ted and Sue wrote their personal articles (testimonials).

- Sue developed the form and instructions for committees.

- Bill wrote articles for the church newsletter on the following topics:

  - The Power of Purpose
  - The Cycle of Empowering
  - Principles Help Us Keep the Faith

Conclusion

Now it's your turn. Build your plan for empowering your congregation. "You are the salt of the earth." Use as much or as little of this process as you deem useful. To positively paraphrase Pogo, "We have met the leaders and they are we."

Epilogue

A central purpose of all the world's religions is to empower the experience of the divine in the lives of the devout. Such empowering occurs in a myriad of ways. Our epiphanies, our struggles, our successes, our defeats, our gains, our losses, our insights, our puzzlements, our intimacy, our loneliness, our light and our darkness can all kindle the gifts within us. It is our hope that the empowering processes you have encountered in this book have stimulated your creative energies and given you permission to see yourselves as instruments of empowering—your self, your relationships, your families, your congregations and your world.

People of faith have been given a task like that of no other institution of society—the task of making love real and palpable in every dimension of life—from social justice to nurturing the young, from giving hope to the dying to inspiring the living. Though the tasks may seem daunting, remember the words of the poet Antonio Machado, "We make the road by walking."

On the following pages you will find session outlines and sample forms. These are meant to guide you in designing your congregation's empowering process. Use them to guide you in developing forms and processes that fit your particular congregation.

Developing Your Congregational Target

In this process you will be compiling the target information you have developed both personally and in your team into a congregational target. When your congregational target is complete you will have:

1. A congregational mission statement
2. Key words for each segment of the target

With these in hand:

- Each person can objectively monitor and evaluate the overall performance of the congregation

- You have a way to identify how well things are going and a quick reference to decide what needs to be emphasized.

Instructions: In this process you will need a designated leader and recorder/secretary. The leader's job is best restricted to leading the group through the exercises. The recorder's job will be to fill in the forms.

Session One

1. Begin by having everyone share the Personal Empowering Target they developed and summarize what they have learned in the process. Ask them to state:

a. Their current understanding of the congregations mission (have the recorder write out each person's mission statement)

b. Their personal purpose

c. How they see their personal purpose and the congregational mission are related (The leader should come prepared to begin this process.)

2. Have everyone share the five key words that they have identified for each of the eight segments on their Personal Empowering Target. Go through these one at a time and have the recorder place all the words on charts. When the same word is used by more than one person in the same segment put a mark by it for each time it is mentioned.

3. After you've listed all the words suggested by the team members, the leader will lead the group in the process of reducing these to five key words for each segment of the "Congregation Empowering Target."

4. Next, review the congregational mission statements the team members have shared and create an "interim" congregational working mission statement. If the congregation currently has a mission

statement, discuss it in light of the members' understanding of the mission and modify if necessary. Compose the "working" congregational mission by editing the existing mission statement. Record this mission statement in the Purpose Section on the target form.

5. Prepare a congregational *Empowering Target.*

6. Ask members to keep the compiled *Congregational Empowering Target* where they will see it and review it regularly between now and the next meeting.

Session Two

> Leader Instructions: Using the information from the target prepared at the last meeting, prepare a target and evaluation form for each member of the team.

1. At the beginning of the meeting pass out prepared forms and ask each member of the team to rank their current assessment of the congregation.

2. Ask each team member to share the positive gains they have had during the process thus far. Discuss ideas for implementing empowering throughout the congregation. Have the secretary record these reports and ideas and compile and distribute them prior to the next meeting.

3. Instruct members to keep the target before them and review it regularly between now and the next meeting.

Session Three

> Instructions: Using the notes on congregational implementation collected in other meetings,

1. Develop a plan to introduce the congregation to the empowering target.

2. Encourage everyone to use the target regularly for personal and congregational assessment.

3. Review and update the target regularly.

4. Make assignments for implementation.

Questions that will help in building a plan:

   • *How will we present and interpret this target to the membership?*

   • *How can we initiate a process by which all or a significant percentage of members can evaluate the congregation regularly?*

   • *What can we do so that members keep the congregational empowering target before them?*

Building Your Congregational Management Principles

The final step in empowering congregations is to articulate the principles by which the congregation agrees to manage life and work. As stated, the three dimensions of quality management are:

1. Purpose-focus

2. Improvement-oriented

3. Principle-management

By now, you can see how being purpose-focused and improvement-oriented empowers you and your team. Establishing management principles serves an equally important role. Once this has happened you'll have mutually developed, agreed-upon principles to guide you in making make difficult decisions. In the words of contemporary management jargon: "You will all be reading off the same page."

To begin this phase of your work it is necessary for all involved to understand the roles of manager and leader. Further, you'll need to accept that you are both managers and leaders in the congregation. The following concepts need to be read and discussed by the team before you begin to build congregational management principles.

Managers and Leaders

There is no question that we are both managers and leaders. Even when we place ourselves in submission to an higher authority, we still have responsibilities for fulfilling mission revealed. Further, we must make decisions that advance and fulfill that mission. Therefore, the question we need to ask is, "Do we manage and lead in a conscious manner?"

Unconscious leadership and management is hit-and-miss at best and confusing and unclear at worst. Awareness of our leadership and management processes provides clarity.

Why are management principles essential? Few argue with the premise that quality outcomes are determined by management and leadership. However, in congregations we are often led to believe that management and leadership are the jobs of a select, empowered and gifted few. Our choices are either to go along with leadership and management, resist it or abandon the organization.

These are not the only options. We can also create a climate where leadership and management are the responsibilities of everyone. It is upon this premise that this concept is built. Plato said, "Society is your name writ large." What we are saying is, "Congregations are your name writ large."

Leadership draws energy from the future–the mission and vision. Management draws energy from the tasks at hand–programs, projects and problems. Whether we realize it or not, in the day-to-day issues we face and the decisions we make, we manage the life of the congregation. Therefore, to achieve quality outcomes, the need for clear and explicit management principles is essential. With such we can select goals and objectives that advance our purpose and fulfill our mission.

Management principles guide the selection of the goals and objectives that we deem will fulfill our mission and are worthy of our effort. Like our personal empowering processes, we have ingrained, semi-conscious, management processes which we utilize to keep the organization going. Ultimately our management principles establish consistency and congruence throughout the many activities of congregational life. By precisely identifying management principles and making them explicit, we develop a clear way to select our goals and objectives and choose actions that we calculate will advance and ultimately fulfill our mission.

W. Edwards Deming developed management principles to insure quality outcomes in business. Using Deming's insights, we can develop our congregational management principles. At first these seem a bit abstract, maybe even farfetched, but that is often true with profound ideas. Just as principles guide us in developing effective organizations, so they can be adapted for developing effective congregations.

A well-established principle of effective group leadership posits that a group functions well when every member of the group knows where they stand with the leader. For the congregation, the principles let people know explicitly how to make decisions based on the goals and principles of the community of faith. The following example illustrates one congregation's use of this process.

Here is an example of the management principles one congregation developed and their methods of implementation.

First Church's Congregational Management Principles

1. Our mission is to bring "good news" through every task we do inside and outside the congregation.

2. Our philosophy is to constantly seek to include everyone, offering comfort, guidance and assistance through all our work.

3. We will evaluate ourselves by our sense of spiritual growth.

4. We will focus our attention on those things that nurture our spiritual growth.

5. We will constantly deepen our understanding of service.

6. We will promote programs that increase our skills in spiritual development.

7. We will keep before us a vision of spiritual harmony.

8. We will use love as our motivating force – not fear, duty or guilt.

9. We will eliminate superficial barriers of class, gender and race from our thinking and actions.

10. We will seek to divine the truth.

11. We will evaluate our effectiveness by the quality of our life and service.

12. We will share our successes regularly and will be open to new experiences that train us to do the work of the congregation.

13. We will be pro-active.

To Implement These Principles We Agree to ...

1. Meditate regularly upon the meaning of each principle in our personal devotional life.

2. Read through these principles as we begin each committee, organization and board meeting.

3. Rate how well we did with each principle at the close of all meetings and services on the congregational evaluation form we have developed.

4. Develop programs that would fulfill these principles.

5. Review and refine our principles annually at our congregational planning retreat.

In Order to Implement and Achieve These Principles We Ask Every Department of the Congregation to ...

1. Review the principles at the beginning of every activity.

2. Rank how well they are doing in each area at the close of each activity and report to the executive committee.

Developing Your Congregational Principles

Session One: Preparing a First Draft of the Congregation's Management Principles

Instructions:

• Write the congregational mission on a board at the front of the room and ask the group to brainstorm for 30 minutes on the principles they would like to see adopted. Write them on the board.

- Ask each member to make up a list of management principles for the congregation and place them in rank-order.

Session Two: Preparing a Final Draft of the Congregational Management Principles and Creating a Working Plan for Implementation

Instructions: Prepare a chart with the Congregational Mission written at the top and the management principles compiled from the last meeting.

- Discuss the principles and do any editing required.
- Rank-order the principles by consensus.
- Ask if there is anything on the board that any member disagrees with. Discuss until you reach a consensus (which could mean editing – or dropping items).
- Share ideas for implementation in the congregation and record these ideas.
- Create a congregational evaluation form (sample below) and use it to evaluate the congregation.

Sample Evaluation Form

First Church's Congregational Management Principles

1. Our mission is to bring "good news" through every task we do inside and outside the congregation

0% _____ 25% _____ 50% _____ 75% _____ 100% _____
(UNFULFILLED)   (FULFILLED)

2. Our philosophy is constantly to seek to include everyone, offering comfort, guidance and assistance through all the work we do.

0% _____ 25% _____ 50% _____ 75% _____ 100% _____
(UNFULFILLED)   (FULFILLED)

3. We will evaluate ourselves by our sense of spiritual growth.

0% _____ 25% _____ 50% _____ 75% _____ 100% _____
(UNFULFILLED)   (FULFILLED)

4. We will focus our attention on those things that nurture our spiritual growth.

0% _____ 25% _____ 50% _____ 75% _____ 100% _____
(UNFULFILLED)   (FULFILLED)

5. We will constantly deepen our understanding of service.

0% _____ 25% _____ 50% _____ 75% _____ 100% _____
(UNFULFILLED)   (FULFILLED)

6. We will promote programs that increase our skills in spiritual development.

0% _____ 25% _____ 50% _____ 75% _____ 100% _____
(UNFULFILLED)   (FULFILLED)

7. We will keep before us a vision of spiritual harmony.

0% _____ 25% _____ 50% _____ 75% _____ 100% _____
(UNFULFILLED)   (FULFILLED)

8. We will use love as our motivating force—not fear.

0% _____ 25% _____ 50% _____ 75% _____ 100% _____
(UNFULFILLED)   (FULFILLED)

9. We will eliminate superficial barriers of class, gender and race from our thinking and actions.

0% _____ 25% _____ 50% _____ 75% _____ 100% _____
(UNFULFILLED)   (FULFILLED)

10. We will seek to divine the truth.

0% _____ 25% _____ 50% _____ 75% _____ 100% _____
(UNFULFILLED)   (FULFILLED)

11. We will evaluate our effectiveness by the quality of our life and service.

0% _____ 25% _____ 50% _____ 75% _____ 100% _____
(UNFULFILLED)   (FULFILLED)

12. We will share our successes regularly.

0% _____ 25% _____ 50% _____ 75% _____ 100% _____
(UNFULFILLED)   (FULFILLED)

13. We will be open to new experiences that train us to do the work of the congregation.

0% _____ 25% _____ 50% _____ 75% _____ 100% _____
(UNFULFILLED)   (FULFILLED)

Sample Forms Developed by Bill's Team

Form #1 – Sally's Form for Committees

Memo to: All Committee Chairs
From: Sally
Re: Empowering Committees

Explanation and instructions: In order to better understand how the work of your committee advances the congregational mission and your personal life purpose, please fill out the front side of this form before each meeting. At the close of the meeting fill out the back side and discuss this with each other.

Form #2 – Empowering Form

(Front Side)
Congregational Purpose:

Committee Purpose:

Meeting Purpose:

Personal Life Purpose:

How Do These Purposes Relate?

(Back Side)

Instructions: Fill in and discuss.

How did today's meeting advance your life purpose?

How did today's meeting advance the life of the congregation?

On a scale of one to ten, ten being the highest, how would you rank this meeting?

- In light of the congregational mission?
- In light of your personal purpose?

Form #3

Table of Contents for the Congregational Empowering Manual

I. The Mission of the Congregation

II. The Congregation's Empowering Target

III. The Congregation's Empowering Map

IV. The Congregation's Empowering Plan

V. The Congregation's Management Principles

VI. Message from the Board of Directors

Form #4

Table of Contents for Members' Empowering Workbook

I. Personal Life Purpose

II. The Congregational Mission

III. How Personal Purpose and Congregational Mission Relate

IV. Personal Empowering Target

V. Congregational Empowering Target

VI. Personal Empowering Map

VII. Congregational Empowering Map

VIII. Personal Empowering Plan

Form #5

Congregational Empowering Plan

Note: This is the plan Bill, Ted and Fred prepared for implementation.

Step One

- Explain to the board of directors the leadership team's experience with the Empowering Process.
- Propose that the congregation enter into a year of empowering.

Step Two (To begin when board and congregational approval have been received.)

- Introduce the concept of empowering with articles and sermons over a three-month period.
- Arrange Empowering classes for all leaders over a three-month period.
- Arrange classes for the membership over a three-month period
- Develop a Congregational Empowering Manual over a three-month period
- Assign a task force to assist leaders and members in implementing the empowering process into the life and work of the congregation.